Please accept this book.
With the compliments of the Canadian Pugwash Group.

William Epstein

Chairman.

We Can Avert

a Nuclear War

We Can Avert

a Nuclear War

edited by

William Epstein

and

Lucy Webster

 Oelgeschlager, Gunn & Hain, Publishers, Inc.
Cambridge, Massachusetts

International Standard Book Number: 0–89946–204–9

Library of Congress Catalog Card Number: 83–4068

Printed in the U.S.A.

Library of Congress Cataloging in Publication Data
Main entry under title:

We can avert a nuclear war.

  Proceedings of the 25th anniversary commemorative meeting of the Pugwash Conference on Science and World Affairs, held in 1982 in Pugwash, N.S.
  Includes index.
  1. Atomic weapons and disarmament—Congresses.
2. Security, International—Congresses.   3. Pugwash Conference on Science and World Affairs.   I. Epstein, William.   II. Webster, Lucy.   III. Pugwash Conference on Science and World Affairs.
JX1974.7.W38   1983   327.1′74   83–4068
ISBN 0-89946-204-9

Contents

FOREWORD

Alfonso Garcia Robles

It is a particular pleasure for me to write a foreword to this volume which sets out the thought-provoking statements of a number of leading scholars in the field of arms control, disarmament and international security, and the vigorous and informative discussions which followed them. As a long-time member of the Pugwash Movement it is an added pleasure to have been able to participate in this 25th Anniversary Commemorative Meeting in Pugwash, Nova Scotia, where the Pugwash Movement was born, and which was made possible by Mrs. Cyrus Eaton and the Canadian Pugwash Group.

The main purpose of the Pugwash Movement is the avoidance of nuclear war. That goal seems as tenuous and far off today as it was 25 years ago, and the danger of a nuclear holocaust, if anything, appears to be much greater today than it was then. Relations between the two superpowers, the United States and the Soviet Union, are equally, if not more strained than they were in 1957, and communication between them is not much better. Each of them has an unimaginable nuclear overkill capability that could destroy them both and the whole world many times over.

Between them, the superpowers have some 50,000 nuclear weapons with more than one million times the power of the small, primitive atom bomb that destroyed Hiroshima. And yet each of them is engaged in a senseless and apparently endless nuclear arms race to modernize and add to their already obscenely excessive overkill capacity. Although most experts agree that there is "rough parity" or "substantial equivalence" between the two superpowers, each of them claims that it must continue arming in order to catch up with the other or prevent it from achieving nuclear superiority. But in existing and all presently forseeable circumstances, where each side has, and will have, sufficient retaliatory power to utterly destroy the other, no matter which one launches a first nuclear strike, the idea of nuclear superiority is not only illusory but absurd.

What is worse, in the past few years concepts and doctrines have been developed and enunciated which visualize the use of nuclear weapons not for deterrence but in order to wage and "win" a nuclear war or, to use a new euphemism, to "prevail" in such a war.

The continued accumulation of more accurate, more powerful and more destabilizing weapons, some of them, such as the cruise missile, so small and mobile that their numbers are incapable of verification, coupled with the new notions of prevailing in a nuclear war, only serves to make a nuclear holocaust all the more possible and, indeed, likely.

Four years ago, the United Nations, at the First Special Session devoted to disarmament, adopted by consensus a Final Document that contained a declaration of principles and a program of action for disarmament, and established the deliberative and negotiating machinery for implementing the program. This result was hailed by the American representative as "a miracle, and no small miracle." In the four years since then, however, no progress was realized in carrying out that program. In fact the world has fallen behind and the situation has worsened. The nuclear arms race has intensified, military expenditures have escalated, the SALT II treaty has not been ratified, the negotiations to achieve a comprehensive test ban treaty—a relatively simple but important measure to halt the nuclear arms race and on which agreement was within reach—have been suspended for the indefinite future, and the current negotiations seem to be stalled, while the arms race continues apace.

The United Nations Second Special Session on Disarmament failed to agree on what was rightly considered the main item of its agenda: the Comprehensive Program of Disarmament. It will have to try again at its 38th regular session, taking as a basis a revised draft to be prepared in 1983 by the Committee on Disarmament, as provided for in the Concluding Document of the Special Session. The same document contained a "unanimous and categorical reaffirmation by all Member States of the validity of the Final Document" of the First Special Session on Disarmament, as well as "their solemn commitment to it and their pledge to respect the priorities in disarmament negotiations as agreed to in its Programme of Action." The Assembly was also able to reach consensus on the World Disarmament Campaign which was officially launched by the President at its opening meeting and which may prove to be a powerful instrument for mobilizing public opinion on behalf of arms limitation and disarmament.

Since no major power appears to be really interested in disarmament, at least in the sense of putting forward significant or far-reaching proposals that have any chance of acceptance by the other side, it would seem that the initiation of the Campaign may well turn out to be one of the most important decisions ever taken by the United Nations in the field of disarmament. If it is carried out in an adequate manner, it can generate the necessary political will of governments to halt and reverse the arms race.

The session also brought to the fore two relatively new issues—a freeze of nuclear weapons and the no-first-use of nuclear weapons—and served to elevate them to the top of the international agenda for disarmament. These two issues may become two of the most important subjects of discussion and negotiation in the 1980s, together with the comprehensive test ban, the prevention of an arms race in outer space and the elimination of chemical weapons.

With regard to the comprehensive test ban—i.e., the extension of the ban on all tests in the atmosphere, in outer space and under water, contained in the 1963 partial Test Ban Treaty, to include also an end to all underground tests—it can be safely stated that no other nuclear arms limitation agreement has been so long sought, and with so much dedication, by the non-nuclear countries of the world, aligned and non-aligned. It is regarded by most of them as the single most important first step towards halting and reversing the nuclear arms race. It is also regarded as a litmus test of the intentions of the nuclear powers to halt the nuclear arms race.

Over the course of some 20 years, all the scientific and technical aspects of the question have been so fully explored that only a political decision is necessary to achieve agreement. The United States, the Soviet Union and the United Kingdom were very close to it in their tripartite negotiations in Geneva for a comprehensive test ban when they were suspended in 1980. The United States decided recently not to resume these negotiations, and in the Committee on Disarmament has attempted to limit any negotiations to the question of verification despite the clear legal obligation contained in both the 1963 Test Ban Treaty and the 1968 Non-Proliferation Treaty.

A comprehensive test ban would curb the nuclear arms race in its most dangerous form—the testing and developing of new technologically advanced and more dangerous nuclear weapons. It is also the best way of preventing the further spread of nuclear weapons.

As to the nuclear freeze, the United States and the Soviet Union should immediately start negotiations to achieve agreement on a mutual and verifiable freeze on the testing, production and deployment of all nuclear weapons and delivery vehicles as a first step towards agreement for substantial reductions of these weapons and their delivery vehicles.

The two superpowers are already legally bound by the Non-Proliferation Treaty to pursue negotiations for the cessation of the nuclear arms race, which means stopping or halting it, or in other words freezing it at its current levels. Given the present situation of rough nuclear parity between the two powers, an across-the-board freeze should be much easier to negotiate and to verify than an agreement for reduction of specific weapons systems. Moreover, without a nuclear freeze, any negotiations or agreement at the START talks for a reduction in strategic nuclear weapons and delivery vehicles would be largely meaningless as it would permit the continued modernization, production and deployment of more dangerous and destabilizing weapons than now exist, such as the MX, the Trident and cruise missiles. A freeze would facilitate and promote the achievement of early agreement on the substantial reduction of nuclear weapons and their delivery systems.

Unilateral initiatives may prove very useful in this case. History has shown that negotiations for disarmament are an extremely slow, cumbersome and protracted process that is often overtaken by the rapid pace of weapons development. Hence it is far better to begin any negotiations by either a simultaneous mutual moratorium by the two powers or by reciprocal unilateral national action. Such reciprocal national actions, which would be subject to verification and be, originally, for an agreed limited period of time, would be the quickest and best way to achieve a comprehensive test ban, a freeze, or almost any other measure of arms limitation or disarmament, pending the outcome of negotiations to achieve a treaty.

The negotiations for strategic arms reductions (START) and those concerning intermediate-range nuclear forces in Europe (INF) would be greatly facilitated by a nuclear freeze. A freeze would demonstrate the serious intentions of the parties to achieve real reductions, and would ensure that the reductions agreed on were not aborted or made meaningless by the production and deployment of more dangerous new or modernized weapons.

The pledges of no-first-use of nuclear weapons undertaken jointly or unilaterally (as have already been made by China and the USSR) would be a major step in the direction of preventing a nuclear war. If made by all the nuclear powers, they would have the same effect as pledges never to use these weapons at all. Such pledges would also facilitate agreement on a nuclear freeze and on reductions of nuclear weapons. They would lead to a relaxation of tension and reduce the risk of accidental war, and of the escalation of conventional and local wars. The making of such pledges by all the nuclear powers would be an important step towards halting and reversing the arms race.

The Outer Space Treaty of 1967 already bans the orbiting or stationing of nuclear weapons in outer space. But not all weapons are banned and dangerous new technologies are being explored and experimented with, that utilize forms of energy other than nuclear. Such technologies involve conventional weapons, lasers and particle beams that could have extremely destabilizing and disastrous effects. They could make outer space a new environment for warfare with incalculable results. It is of great importance to stop their development before it is too late.

Here again the situation could be frozen and the freeze on outer space weapons could also be initiated by simultaneous or joint national action, as was done in 1963 when the United States and the USSR declared their intention not to station nuclear or other mass destruction weapons in outer space. This joint national action by the two powers led to the early conclusion of the Outer Space Treaty.

Any one of the above measures would constitute a major step towards halting and reversing the nuclear arms race. Taken together they would constitute a significant contribution to the prevention of nuclear war and the ultimate elimination of all nuclear weapons.

PREFACE

The Pugwash Movement started with the Manifesto issued by Bertrand Russell and Albert Einstein in London, England, in 1955, after the explosion of the first hydrogen bombs by the United States and the Soviet Union. They called on the scientists of the world to come together and to urge governments to renounce war rather than to follow a course that could put an end to the human race.

The first conference was held in the village of Pugwash, Nova Scotia, in 1957, at the invitation of Mr. Cyrus Eaton, and brought together scientists from East and West with the aim of preventing nuclear incineration. That conference was attended by 22 scientists from 10 countries.

The Pugwash Movement was born at that first Pugwash Conference. This was during the dark days of the Cold War when there was very little communication between East and West—either on the governmental or the non-governmental level. But the Pugwash scientists decided to meet again and to continue to communicate with each other and with other scientists to exert concerted efforts with a view to help reduce the threat of nuclear war. Since that time the Movement has spread around the world and now encompasses some 2000 scientists including a number of Nobel Laureates in 75 countries. In fact the word "Pugwash" is now included in the Oxford English Dictionary where it is described as denoting the "international conferences of eminent scientists to discuss world problems" and that the name came from Pugwash, Nova Scotia, where the first conference was held.

Since its founding, the Pugwash Movement has held more than 30 major international conferences in various world centers, and some three dozen symposiums and many workshops, where learned experts grappled with specific world problems of war and peace and came forward with conclusions and recommendations. These were conveyed to governments, to other scientists and to the interested public as a contribution towards avoiding war, and above all a nuclear war, and achieving international peace.

Today there is once again a worsening of relations beween East and West, a significant increase in tensions, and a notable decrease in communication. The role for Pugwash is as great today as it was when the Movement started.

Mrs. Cyrus Eaton and the Canadian Pugwash Group decided to hold a Commemorative Meeting at Pugwash on the 25th anniversary of the first Pugwash Conference to assess how far we have come in the quarter of a century, where we are now and where we should be going.

The meeting attracted a number of distinguished scientists, including the two surviving signatories of the Russell-Einstein Manifesto, and five of the participants at the first Pugwash Conference. By deliberate choice, the participants included not only scientists and experts outside of governments but also a number of political figures and diplomats who play an active and leading role in the disarmament negotiations. In this way, it was intended that the discussions should promote an interplay of ideas and experience, of the ideal and the practical, and result in concrete pragmatic proposals for action.

The commemorative statements, and the detailed discussions which followed, introduced and developed several new and important approaches to halting the nuclear arms race and enhancing international security. These included currently topical questions such as the nuclear freeze, the no-first-use of nuclear weapons, the World Disarmament Campaign, the role of scientists and the public, the banning of weapons from outer space and the establishment of an international satellite monitoring system. They also analyzed the policies and actions of the Reagan Administration with regard to the arms race and the arms control negotiations, and urged the usefulness of the two superpowers taking unilateral initiatives and national actions, on a reciprocal basis, to halt and reverse the spiraling arms race. The participants unanimously supported a Declaration by the Canadian Pugwash Group on the current state of the world and proposals to improve it.

Because of the importance and topicality of the subjects and the discussion, and the surging public anti-nuclear war movement, it was decided that the statements and a summary of the discussion and the proposals made should be published. It was hoped that these might provide some insights and guidance to an understanding of the complex and controversial issues of the arms race and arms control, and could be put to practical use by government leaders, legislators, non-governmental organizations, scientists, members of the public and all persons interested in avoiding war and promoting peace.

Ambassador Alfonso Garcia Robles was an active participant in the Commemorative Meeting. In October 1982 it was announced that he and Mrs. Alva Myrdal of Sweden were jointly awarded the 1982 Nobel Peace Prize. Alfonso Garcia Robles has written the Foreword for this volume with a penetrating analysis of the current arms race and of the international situation, which makes some important and timely suggestions for coping with them. His suggestions can help the nations of the world to end the present stalemate in the negotiations for arms limitation and disarmament and to reverse the dangerous trend in the relations between two superpowers.

The discussions were detailed and the issues often hotly debated. The summaries of the remarks are attributed to the speaker, in the order in which they were made, but some rearrangement was necessary for clarity. Because interventions made by speakers in the discussion were unrehearsed and spontaneous, they provide a directness that is refreshing and unusual in serious scholarly work.

William Epstein

Acknowledgments

I must express my great thanks to Mrs. Cyrus Eaton and the Pugwash Park Commissioners for their continuing support, both financial and moral, for the Canadian Pugwash Group and for the objectives of the Pugwash Movement. The thanks of all participants go to them and to their assistants for the excellence of their hospitality and of the services provided at the 25th Anniversary Commemorative Meeting at Pugwash.

I owe a particular debt of gratitude to my co-editor Lucy Webster who undertook the primary task of editing the speeches and the sometimes confusing discussions with exceptional skill and perceptivity. Her interest in and knowledge of the subject contributed greatly to the clarity of the text.

Finally, my warm thanks and appreciation must be registered to the Cyrus Eaton Foundation of Cleveland, Ohio, to the Walter and Duncan Gordon Charitable Foundation of Toronto, Ontario, to the Pugwash Park Commission of Pugwash, Nova Scotia, and to the Disarmament Fund of the Department of External Affairs of the Government of Canada for their generous financial support that made possible the publication and wide distribution of this book.

HEAD TABLE OF THE PUGWASH
COMMEMORATIVE SESSION

(left to right)
Anne Eaton, William Epstein, The Honorable Mark MacGuigan, Ambassador Alexander Yakovlev.

Photo by Susan Brenciaglia.

PARTICIPANTS

Dr. G. Brenciagla
  Manager, Fuel and Physics Department
  Ontario Hydro
  Toronto, Ontario, Canada
  Commissioner, Pugwash Park Commissioners

Mr. Fox Butterfield
  New York Times
  15 Court Square
  Boston, Mass. 02181, U.S.A.

Prof. Rod Byers
  Department of Political Science
  York University
  Downsview, Ontario, Canada

Dr. Paul Cappon
  Director of Medical Services
  Halifax, Nova Scotia, Canada

Dr. Ian Carr
  St. Boniface General Hospital
  409 Tache Ave.
  Winnipeg, Manitoba, Canada

Prof. David F. Cavers
  Harvard Law School
  Cambridge, Mass. 02138, U.S.A.

Prof. Paul Doty
  Director, Center for Science
    and International Affairs
  Harvard University
  Cambridge, Mass. 02138, U.S.A.

Mrs. Cyrus Eaton
  Pugwash, Nova Scotia
  Chairman, Pugwash Park Commissioners

William Epstein

Chairman, Canadian Pugwash
Special Fellow, UNITAR, United Nations
New York, N.Y. 10017, U.S.A.
Former Director of Disarmament
at the United Nations

Prof. Bernard Feld

Physics Department
Massachusetts Institute of Technology
Cambridge, Mass. 02139, U.S.A.
Editor-in-Chief
The Bulletin of the Atomic Scientists

Dr. Margaret Fulton

President, Mt. St. Vincent University
166 Bedford Highway
Halifax, Nova Scotia, Canada

Ambassador A. Garcia Robles

Mexican Representative
to the Committee on Disarmament
Geneva, Switzerland
Former Minister of Foreign Affairs of Mexico
Nobel Peace Prize Laureate, 1982

Mr. James George

Threshold Foundation Bureau of America
197 South Road
Chester, N.J. 07930
Former Canadian High Commissioner to India
and Ambassador to Iran

Rev. Theodore Hesburgh, CSC

President, University of Notre Dame
Notre Dame, Indiana 46556, U.S.A.

Mr. Tomosaburu Hirano

Associate Editor
The Seikyo Shimbun
Tokyo, Japan

Dr. George Ignatieff

Chancellor, University of Toronto
Toronto, Canada
Former Canadian Representative to NATO,
the United Nations, and to the
Committee on Disarmament

Prof. Sergei Kapitza

Academy of Sciences
14 Leninsky Prospekt
Moscow, USSR
Moderator of General Science Program
for USSR Television

Miss Flora Lewis

New York Times
3 rue Scribe
Paris 75009, France

Ambassador James Leonard

Chairman of the Board
The Committee on National Security
1570 34th Street, N.W.
Washington, D.C. 20007
Former U.S. Representative
to the Committee on Disarmament

The Hon. Mark MacGuigan

Secretary of State for External Affairs
Ottawa, Ontario, Canada

Prof. Iwao Ogawa

Department of Physics
Rikkyo University
Tokyo, Japan

Sir Mark Oliphant

37 Colvin Street
Hughes, Canberra, Australia
Professor Emeritus, Institute of Advanced
Studies, Canberra University

Prof. Derek Paul

Department of Physics
University of Toronto
Toronto, Ontario, Canada

Dr. Linus Pauling

Linus Pauling Institute
440 Page Mill Road
Palo Alto, Calif. 94306, U.S.A.
Nobel Laureate for Peace and for Chemistry
A signatory of the Russell-Einstein Manifesto

Prof. John C. Polanyi

University Professor
Lash Miller Laboratories
University of Toronto
Toronto, Ontario, Canada

Mr. Robert Reford

12 Metcalfe Street
Toronto, Ontario, Canada
Co-convenor,
    Canadian Disarmament Study Group

Prof. Joseph Rotblat

8 Asmara Road
London, England
A signatory of the Russel-Einstein Manifesto
First Secretary-General
    of the Pugwash Movement

Miss Betty Royon

Secretary at the First Pugwash Conference
Hudson, Ohio, U.S.A.

Mr. Herbert Scoville, Jr.

President, Arms Control Association
11 Dupont Circle
Washington, D.C. 20036, U.S.A.
Former Deputy Director of
    U.S. Arms Control and Disarmament Agency
    and of the Central Intelligence Agency

Dr. Frank Sommers

> President
> Canadian Physicians
>   for Social Responsibility
> 3600 Bloor Street West
> Toronto, Ontario, Canada

Mr. K. Subrahmanyan

> Director
> Institute for Defense Studies and Analyses
> New Delhi, India

Mr. William Swartz

> 1430 West Wrightswood Avenue
> Chicago, Illinois 60614, U.S.A.
> Executive Director,
>   Albert Einstein Peace Prize Foundation

Mr. Ray Szabo

> CSX Corporation
> Richmond, Virginia 23261, U.S.A.

Mrs. Inga Thorsson

> Under-Secretary of State of Sweden
>   for Disarmament
> Ministry for Foreign Affairs
> Stockholm, Sweden

Mrs. Lucy Webster

> Executive Chairman
> World Association of World Federalists
> 320 East 46th Street
> New York, N.Y. 10017, U.S.A.

Ambassador Alexander N. Yakovlev

> Embassy of the USSR to Canada
> 390 Lisgar Road
> Rockcliffe Park
> Ottawa, Ontario, Canada

PARTICIPANTS IN THE PUGWASH COMMEMORATIVE SESSION

Front Row (left to right): Paul Doty, David Cavers, Inga Thorsson, Joseph Rotblat, Anne Eaton, Sir Mark Oliphant, Iwao Ogawa.

Middle Row (left to right): Linus Pauling, Tomosaburu Hirano, Flora Lewis, George Ignatieff, Lucy Webster, James George, Betty Royon, John Polanyi, William Epstein, Theodore Hesburgh, Margaret Fulton, Derek Paul.

Back Row (left to right): Fox Butterfield, Frank Sommers, James Leonard, K. Subrahmanyan, Giovanni Brenciaglia, Ian Carr, Herbert Scoville, Paul Cappon, Bernard Feld, Alfonso Garcia Robles, William Swartz, Ray Szabo, Sergei Kapitza, Robert Reford, Raymond Bourgue, Rod Byers.

Photo by Stephen Thorne, Halifax Chronicle-Herald.

PART I

The Commemorative Session:

Disarmament and World Affairs

1. WHY THE MEETING TOOK PLACE

Opening Remarks
by the Chairman and Mrs. Cyrus Eaton

William Epstein, Chairman:

This is a great occasion for Pugwash, Nova Scotia, for Canada, and for the Pugwash Movement. In planning this meeting we recognized that the world is in just as bad a mess, or an even worse mess, than it was 25 years ago when Pugwash started. From this little village of less than 1000 souls today, the word went out to many lands and acquired momentum and some measure of influence around the world.

Twenty-five years ago there was almost no communication between East and West and the Pugwash Movement began in an effort to start communication at least between the scientists of East and West to try to prevent a nuclear holocaust. Today communications between East and West seem to have broken down again. Mrs. Cyrus Eaton and I felt it was an opportune moment to hold this 25th anniversary commemorative meeting to stress again the need to re-establish East-West communications. It is opportune also because all the things that are going on in the world, not only as regards the threat of the escalating arms race but also because of the awakening of the people, as evidenced by the millions marching all over Europe and North America and rallying against nuclear war. This meeting was also intended to be a reunion of all the old friends who were here at the beginning. We wanted to have with us the two living signers of the Russell-Einstein Manifesto: Linus Pauling and Joseph Rotblat, and we are very happy that they are here. Also there are five scientists here today who were here in 1957: Sir Mark Oliphant, who came from Australia; David Cavers and Paul Doty who came from Harvard University in Cambridge,

Massachusetts; Professor Iwao Ogawa who came from Japan; and Joseph Rotblat who came from London.

This meeting is also intended to honor the memory of that great man of peace, a man of vision and courage who had the imagination and the foresight to invite the scientists from East and West from 10 countries here in 1957, after the Russell-Einstein Manifesto. I'm sure we all miss him although he was with us a long time. We pay tribute to the memory of Cyrus Eaton. We are delighted that Anne Eaton is carrying on in the same tradition.

Furthermore, we feel that we may even be able to say something once again that will help to continue the tradition that started here 25 years ago. We also wanted this event to be a follow-up to the Banff Pugwash Conference, which was the thirty-first of the international conferences, and the first to be held in Canada in more than twenty years. Finally, we thought it could provide a prelude to the Warsaw Conference which takes place in August, the thirty-second Pugwash Conference. We had hoped at one time that we might persuade other Pugwash national groups to hold similar commemorative meetings in their countries, but we didn't succeed in getting the support of the Pugwash Council for that.

Proof of the importance of this meeting and of the things that we want to say and do here is the fact that the Hon. Mark MacGuigan, the Canadian Secretary of State for External Affairs, left Ottawa late last night, after a vote in the House of Commons, and has to leave at noon so he can get back for another vote at about 3 o'clock this afternoon. Sometimes we think that our lives are a little too hectic! But Mark MacGuigan thought it important enough to go to all that trouble to give us a statement on behalf of Canada.

Anyway, this is a splendid gathering, and Anne Eaton would like to welcome you.

Anne Eaton:

Cyrus Eaton would think this marvellous—that all of you have come here for this meeting. He would be extremely grateful to Bill Epstein and the Canadians for organizing it; he would feel that the presence of Mr. MacGuigan has really put Pugwash on the map. I am so grateful to all of you for coming.

I have over here on the wall, pictures, candid shots, of the first meeting in 1957. I particularly want to point out to Ambassador Yakovlev and Mr. Kapitza, because I'm so proud of it, that we have "Pugwash" written in Russian as well as in English. That is one of the things that Pugwash is all about.

I hope you will all find this conference as disarming and stimulating as the first one.

Message from the Prime Minister of Canada

Chairman:

Prime Minister Pierre Elliot Trudeau was not able to join us here, but he has sent us a message which with your permission, Mr. Secretary of State, I would like to read.

It is with much pleasure that I extend greetings to all in attendance at the twenty-fifth Anniversary Meeting of the Pugwash Movement.

A quarter of a century ago, distinguished world scientists, in reaction to their concern about the consequences of the buildup of nuclear armaments, responded to the invitation of Cyrus Eaton to attend the first Pugwash Conference.

No one doubts that their concern was well-founded, for since that time the dangers of nuclear war have increased significantly, with nation after nation scrambling to arm themselves with weapons of awesome destructive force.

The world is living under a cloud of insecurity, suspicion, violence and disorder unparalleled in its history. We must find the means whereby multi-lateral reductions in nuclear arms can be effected, and maintained. This in turn demands a sure method of verification, for only measures that offer mutual security are likely to offer solutions to present tensions.

I regret my inability to be present during your important discussions. May they prove thought-provoking and fruitful.

Message from the United Nations Secretary-General

We have also had a message from the new Secretary-General of the United Nations, Javier Perez de Cuellar.

On the occasion of the 25th Anniversary Commemorative meeting of the Pugwash Movement, I send you my best wishes. The founders of the Pugwash Movement and those who have come after them have dedicated themselves to many of the fundamental aims to which the activities of the United Nations are devoted. Pugwash has played an important catalytic role in the field of arms limitation and disarmament which has also widened the awareness of many who are now concerned with the survival of humanity. I know of the conviction and devotion with which Pugwash pursues these objectives. It is therefore with great pleasure that I am sending you my best wishes on this memorable occasion.

We have five items on our agenda.

1. Declaration on the 25th Anniversary of Pugwash.

2. The World Disarmament Campaign:
   Mobilizing Public Opinion

3. The Nuclear Freeze

4. The Future of Disarmament and a Nuclear Freeze

5. The Political Role of Scientists and the
   Pugwash Movement

These topics will certainly be dealt with in some of the commemorative addresses today, but we shall discuss them in greater detail and depth tomorrow.

Instead of delivering a speech, I shall confine myself to reading to you a declaration that has been provisionally approved by the Canadian Pugwash Group. We shall circulate the text and have an opportunity to consider and improve it this afternoon.

We shall now begin with the commemorative addresses by our distinguished guests.

2. THE WORLD DISARMAMENT PICTURE:

A CANADIAN PERSPECTIVE

Mark MacGuigan

I must say that one of the sorrows of being a transplanted academic in politics is not being able to linger to hear the actual discussion which takes place, and I'll be looking to Bill Epstein subsequently for a blow by blow account of the discussions that you have. I'd much rather be down there listening than up here delivering this, and I am sorry that I have to rush off. When I originally planned this, I had hoped to be here for the entire meeting. I wasn't then expecting a cabinet meeting and a vote this afternoon.

A twenty-fifth anniversary is a very special occasion. It is a time both for reflection and for looking at the future. Characteristically, the Pugwash Movement will, I feel certain, tend to look ahead, as I propose to do today.

I am delighted to join with you in commemorating the first Pugwash Conference held here in Pugwash, Nova Scotia in 1957 at the invitation of Mr. Cyrus Eaton. I commend the initiative of Mrs. Eaton and the Canadian Pugwash Group in convening this silver anniversary meeting. Today, as never before, people throughout the world are increasingly concerned about the spiralling arms race and are looking not only to governments but to groups such as yours to generate possible new approaches to the complex issues of arms control and disarmament.

The founding of the Pugwash Movement anticipated this increased public interest in the subject of arms control and disarmament, and probably led it. The manifesto issued by Bertrand Russell and Albert Einstein called on governments to renounce war rather than to follow a course which could put an end to the human race; the core of people's concern today is exactly that. As Prime Minister Trudeau put it at UNSSOD II, the people of the world "are reminding political leaders that what is at stake is the crucial matter of the life or death of mankind."

The manner in which the Pugwash Movement has spread to embrace distinguished individuals in many countries reflects its importance. In Canada its influence continues to expand in what I consider to be a most significant way, because it is reaching out to the young men and women of our country. I am referring to the birth a year ago of Canadian Student Pugwash, which held a well-organized and successful first conference in Ottawa and, a few weeks ago, an Atlantic Regional Conference in Halifax. The Canadian Government was pleased to offer assistance for both of these conferences, as it did for your conference in Banff last summer.

During the next two days you will undoubtedly be discussing the second UN Special Session on Disarmament which ended last week, and also the prospects for the period ahead. I would like to share with you some thoughts on each. In my view, it would be a mistake to dwell too long on what was not achieved at UNSSOD II or to succumb to the temptation of sustained hand-wringing about failure. Rather, we should be grateful that it was held at all in spite of an exceedingly unpropitious international atmosphere.

We should also welcome the fact that UNSSOD II preserved intact the viability of the United Nations system to deliberate constructively on international security matters, particularly arms control and disarmament. Despite the temptation to vote resolutions which could not achieve consensus, the non-aligned countries in the end chose the path of realism rather than a procedure which could only devalue the system.

An important achievement of UNSSOD II was its reaffirmation of the Final Document of UNSSOD I. The program of Action in that Final Document highlighted the importance of the negotiating process, as did the many world leaders who addressed the Special Session.

In his address Prime Minister Trudeau seized the occasion to call again on the nuclear powers to negotiate four verifiable arms control agreements which, in their combination, would halt the technological momentum of the nuclear arms race. They are: a comprehensive nuclear test ban; a ban on the flight-testing of all new strategic delivery vehicles; a ban on the production of fissionable material for weapons purposes; and a limitation and eventual reduction of military spending for new strategic weapons systems. This strategy of suffocation, the Prime Minister stressed, is not in competition with current negotiations on reductions of all nuclear weapons. To underline this point, he proposed that the strategy be enfolded into a policy of stabilization which has two complementary components: the current negotiating approach aimed at achieving a stable nuclear balance at lower levels; and the strategy of suffocation aimed at inhibiting the development of new nuclear weapons systems.

Canadian statements in the working groups and the Committee of the Whole underlined Canada's flexibility and desire to search for consensus language on such agenda items as a comprehensive program of disarmament, enhancement of the effectiveness of disarmament machinery, and a world disarmament campaign. It was a Canadian informal paper which formed the basis of deliberations on a world disarmament campaign, and sustained Canadian efforts played no small part in the consensus achieved on the conduct of the campaign. Canada was also active in its traditional role of chairman of the Barton Group, the informal consultative body of twenty like-minded Western countries. Attached to the Delegation were nineteen parliamentary observers and fifteen consultants drawn from non-governmental organizations and universities. In addition, the Canadian Delegation provided regular briefings for members of Canadian non-governmental organizations attending the Special Session.

Although the second Special Session on Disarmament did not achieve all that many people and governments hoped it would, it did serve to focus attention on the crucial and often complex arms control and disarmament issues of our time. It also served, I believe, to underline the extent to which an exceedingly heavy responsibility rests with those countries which have embarked on serious arms control negotiations.

While the picture may not appear as bright as many would like, I am nevertheless hopeful about the future. I believe that the superpowers themselves want to avoid moving in the direction of nuclear confrontation and that each can see national interests being served by agreements.

Why, you may ask skeptically, am I so persuaded?

First, the existence of nuclear weapons and the incalculable consequences of their use, even on a limited scale, have proved to be an effective deterrent for over 30 years. The fact that either side can now absorb a first strike and still respond with devastating effect has caused each side to proceed with caution and to avoid confrontation in time of crisis.

Second, existing agreements are being respected. In accordance with SALT I (which includes the ABM Treaty and the Interim Agreement on Offensive Arms) both the Soviet Union and the United States have taken steps to dismantle strategic systems. The USSR has dismantled a number of "Yankee" class submarines and the USA is dismantling its Polaris subs as new Trident submarines are being put into service.

Third, although considered "badly flawed" by critics, SALT II is being largely implemented by both sides. In a recent speech President Brezhnev expressed his willingness "to preserve" the positive aspects of previous agreements. President Reagan has welcomed President Brezhnev's statement and has indicated that US policy is to take no action that would undercut existing agreements provided the Soviet Union exercises equal restraint.

Finally, two negotiations on nuclear weapons are underway in Geneva. I do not need to rehearse for this specialized audience the details of the positions put forward by the United States, which in the case of intermediate-range nuclear forces have been worked out in consultation with allies, including Canada.

Numerous criticisms have, as you know, been levelled at the Western position in both sets of negotiations, the main one being that by concentrating on those forces where the USSR has superiority the positions are manifestly unfair, if not non-negotiable. My answer to this criticism is two-fold. First, our prime objective is to create a greater degree of stability, and consequently it makes sense to concentrate in the first instance on those systems which have created a high degree of imbalance and are destabilizing—the SS-20s in the European theatre and heavy Soviet ICBMs with multiple warheads in the intercontinental theatre. Second, the United States has made clear in the START talks that other systems of direct concern to the Soviet Union (heavy bombers and submarine-launched ballistic missiles) are negotiable. Most important, the West is seeking in these talks actual reductions. One should not lose sight of the fact that both of the SALT agreements established limits. They did not result in any significant reductions in existing forces, and in some respects allowed the parties to increase up to the agreed limits. Frankly, from the reports I have received to date on the INF and START talks, I am impressed by the serious and businesslike approach of both sides.

The Vienna talks on force reductions in Central Europe are in their ninth year but have so far not attracted much media attention in Canada. While some progress has been made in these negotiations, in which Canada is a direct participant, the principal stumbling block has been the failure to reach agreement in factual terms on the present strength of Warsaw Pact forces. The Soviet Union insists that the total number of WPO forces in the area is almost 150,000 less than the number which has been confirmed by the best allied intelligence available. Continuing efforts have been made by the Western negotiators to persuade the Eastern members to provide a detailed breakdown of their figures to support their calculations or to cooperate in clarifying the differences between Western and Eastern figures. Unless both sides can agree on the numerical base from which reductions must be made, clearly it is virtually impossible to verify what is left after reductions even if such reductions can be monitored. Moreover, the Eastern side has proved to be very reluctant to accept what NATO would regard as adequate verification measures.

New life is being injected into these negotiations through a draft treaty tabled by the West last week in Vienna which makes substantial concessions to the Eastern side. The West now proposes that the countries concerned should undertake a binding obligation in one agreement (instead of two sequential agreements as proposed previously) to reduce to a common collective ceiling on each side of approximately 700,000 ground force manpower and 900,000 ground and air force personnel combined. These reductions would be in four stages over a period of seven years, with the United States and the Soviet Union with-drawing 13,000 and 30,000 troops respectively in the first year after conclusion of the agreement. Other direct participants including Canada would join in the reduction process in the three final stages. Agreement on manpower data would remain a pre-condition. If the Warsaw Pact countries are prepared to cooperate, particularly on the question of the actual present strength of their forces in the area and on verification, it should now be possible to progress more rapidly toward an agreement.

I am certain you would agree that a reduction and balancing of the existing levels of troops of the two Alliances confronting each other in Central Europe would serve to reduce tensions and improve the climate of East-West relations. Such an agreement would also maintain and even enhance the security of the two sides.

The Committee on Disarmament, the multilateral nego-tiating body in Geneva, will resume its 1982 session early next month. Its new Working Group on a Comprehensive Test Ban will begin its work on verification and com-pliance. Its Working Group on Chemical Weapons will build upon previous progress. Another subject to be taken up is that of arms control and outer space. This question is one of special interest to Canada. In his speech to UNSSOD II the Prime Minister drew attention to the serious gaps in the present international agreements and proposed that an early start be made on a treaty to prohibit the develop-ment, testing and deployment of all weapons for use in outer space.

With such an arms control and disarmament agenda— START, INF, MBFR, CD—there are grounds for hope, especially compared to the situation as recently as a year ago when the Pugwash Conference gathered in Banff.

I would like to suggest areas in which the Pugwash Movement might expand its efforts in the years ahead. It should come as no surprise that they are areas of tradition-al importance to Canada.

One of the great strengths of the Pugwash Movement has been its recognition that the promotion of peace and human survival necessarily involves the consideration of all weapons systems. I am thinking in particular of the excellent work over the years in the Pugwash Chemical Weapons Seminars. I consider these meetings to be among the major achievements of the first twenty-five years of the Movement. Ever since the first World War, a ban on chemical weapons has been high on any list of Canadian priorities in arms control and disarmament. In the Committee on Disarmament in Geneva, the same expert who has attended Pugwash Chemical Weapons Seminars has participated with experts from other countries in the Working Group on Chemical Weapons established in 1980. One of the initiatives I announced last week is that henceforth Canadian experts will participate in the Working Group for longer periods as and when warranted. We are convinced that the international negotiating machinery that is in place must be used to achieve a comprehensive ban on chemical weapons. Adequate verification provisions will be among the most important parts of such a treaty. Canada has noted with interest the positive approach to verification procedures in Foreign Minister Gromyko's remarks at UNSSOD II. We would be encouraged if this attitude were reflected in the ongoing negotiations in the CD.

It is my hope that in the next twenty-five years members of your Movement will give even greater attention to chemical weapons and to other non-nuclear weapon systems. Part of the educational task of the Movement is, I believe, to increase public understanding that to attain peace and human survival one must seek to limit and reduce all weapons systems. It would be a tragedy if a result of the understandable and justifiable public concern about *nuclear* weapons were to make *non-nuclear* war more likely. Your business and the business of governments must continue to be the promotion of steps which reduce the likelihood of the use of force—the use of any weapons system.

My second suggestion concerns verification. Prime Minister Trudeau said at the second Special Session that "the international community should address itself to verification as one of the most significant factors in disarmament negotiations in the 1980s." He was, of course, addressing primarily governments. But individuals with expertise and non-governmental organizations also have a vital role to play not only in achieving greater public understanding but also in ensuring that all available expertise is applied to this increasingly complex subject. Since World War II Canada has attached special importance to the development of international verification mechanisms. In recent years the Government has drawn on technical expertise in a number of departments. Further steps are being taken at the present time. We have committed funds to enable Canada to become a member of the international seismic-data exchange, an international verification mechanism being developed in connection with a comprehensive nuclear test ban. In a few months Canada will be joining those countries already exchanging data on a provisional basis. We have called for the early implementation of the Exchange in advance of a treaty.

Within our research and public information program, established after UNSSOD I and substantially increased in size this year, we intend to put special emphasis in the coming year on research projects related to verification by Canadian universities, institutes and individuals.

We will also institutionalize an expanding Canadian role in verification issues in order to utilize effectively expertise in several government departments and in the private sector in the negotiation of agreements on nuclear, chemical and conventional weapons systems. I am referring in particular to expertise in seismology, nuclear safeguards, remote sensing, toxicology and protective measures against chemical weapons, and communication satellites.

There is a third subject, Mr. Chairman, which deserves the attention of the Pugwash Movement in the years ahead. It is horizontal proliferation of nuclear weapons. At UNSSOD II member states including Canada quite rightly concentrated on vertical proliferation. But Canada, as a strong supporter of the Non-Proliferation Treaty, has always insisted that the two cannot be separated in reality. Thus Canadian priorities in arms control and disarmament include the promotion of the evolution of an effective non-proliferation regime based on the NPT.

Canada's non-proliferation policy as it is applied to nuclear exports is intended to inhibit the diversion of nuclear materials for weapons purposes. Our two-tiered approach to the safeguarding of nuclear exports provides a strong lead to the rest of the world.

In the first instance, we require that prospective nuclear partners, if they are non-nuclear weapons states, be parties to the Non-Proliferation Treaty (NPT) or have made equivalent commitments, including "fullscope" safe-guards. Secondly, countries must enter into a bilateral nuclear cooperation agreement with Canada which incorporates, *inter alia*, the provision of "fallback" safeguards. These two requirements combine in a comprehensive, systematic manner and form the foundation of Canadian nuclear export policy, which is applied without discrimination, and under which proliferation cannot occur unless treaty obligations are broken.

Canada's commitment to the use and diffusion of nuclear technology for peaceful purposes continues. Indeed, in the context of a broad Canadian effort to redouble its assistance to developing countries, Canada has recently signed or negotiated nuclear cooperation agreements with Egypt, Indonesia, Mexico and the Philippines, as well as with Sweden, Euratom and Australia. We are currently engaged in an initiative to enlarge cooperation to include regulatory training, the exchange of technical information, and cooperative responses to potential radiation emergencies. It is our hope that this initiative can become a model of technology transfer to strengthen nuclear cooperation with the Third World.

A realistic assessment, however, suggests that Canada has, for the most part, proceeded as far as is feasible on its own in exerting national influence to prevent a spread of nuclear weapons. It is now clear that further progress will be largely contingent upon multilateral agreements under the auspices of the United Nations and the IAEA.

The international community accomplished a significant step forward with the NPT, and we can look back with satisfaction at the fact that there are now some 115 signatories. At the same time, however, it should be recognized that the NPT is an initial treaty and that it needs to be perfected. I hope that in historical terms the NPT will be considered as a watershed, as it has provided the vehicle for a large majority of UN member countries to express formally and for the first time their total renunciation of nuclear weapons and weapons capability. I would also hope that the NPT will spawn new, more comprehensive and more truly universal treaties.

In this regard, it cannot be ignored that although the NPT emphasizes the non-discriminatory transfer of peaceful nuclear tecnology, it also provides, under Article VI, for the rapid and effective movement towards disarmament and the de-escalation of the arms race on the part of nuclear weapons states. The fact that this key element of the NPT remains unfulfilled suggests to me that a tangible move towards disarmament on behalf of the superpowers represents the best possible means to indicate, with sincerity, their belief in the legitimacy of non-proliferation.

Accordingly, in the context of the United Nations and the IAEA, Canada is prepared to seek international consensus on the development of principles which would result in a more universal and effective approach to non-proliferation. Such principles should include a formal renunciation of nuclear explosive devices and an agreement to permit the safeguarding of all nuclear activities throughout the entire range of the nuclear fuel cycle as fundamental to the creation of a stable and permanent non-proliferation regime. Under such conditions, bilateral nuclear commitments could then be subsumed into a truly equitable and responsible international order.

It is my belief that the moment has arrived for genuine movement through collective institutional and policy approaches towards the realization of these objectives. If states fail to engage this challenge in a manner which is both imaginative and just, the prognosis for the uncontrolled horizontal proliferation of nuclear capabilities will remain more of a threat than an opportunity for enhanced international cooperation.

One of the underlying themes of my remarks today has been public understanding, which has been a continuing objective of the Pugwash Movement. The challenge of promoting greater public understanding faces governments and non-governmental organizations alike. In the period between the first and second Special Sessions, there were a number of UN studies designed to improve public understanding. In addition, there was the very thoughtful Report of the Independent Commission on Disarmament and Security Issues chaired by Olof Palme. Canada was active in these endeavours. Robert Ford, the former Canadian Ambassador in Moscow, was a member of the Palme Commission and the Canadian Government made a substantial financial contribution to its work. Canadian experts participated in a number of UN disarmament studies. In the case of the study on the relationship between disarmament and development, the Government also funded the writing of a popular version of the report, which has now been published commercially in French and English and other languages.

I have no quarrel with those who wish to alert our peoples to the potential horrors of a nuclear war. The objective they seek, a world safe from the threat of a nuclear conflict, is the same goal which the Canadian Government pursues by every means at its disposal. We are not always in agreement, however, on how this end can best be achieved. To explain complex negotiating positions to the general public can be exceedingly difficult. Simple declaratory statements are fairly easy to grasp but the potential negative implications for our overall objective— peace and security—are seldom self-evident. Moreover, in my experience, efforts to describe them can often be misunderstood. I very much hope that the Pugwash Movement will play its part, for which it is so eminently suited, in explaining that facile declaratory measures are no substitute for the negotiation of equitable and verifiable arms control and disarmament agreements.

The easy response to the current tensions of the international situation is to argue that only disarmament or only defence fundamentally matters. However, to insist that only one or the other can enhance security and preserve peace is to misunderstand the basic components of security policy. The realistic position is to recognize that disarmament and defence complement and support each other.

Our challenge as responsible internationalists is to search for and discover new approaches to a balanced security policy which will both maintain our dedication to our ideals and enable us to move towards a realizable possibility of world peace.

Chairman:

Thank you very much, Mr. Secretary of State for that very clear statement of the views of the Canadian Government with much of which we are in full agreement. I think I would not be revealing any great secret to you if I mention that the priorities of the Canadian Government and those of the Pugwash Movement are not identical but are very similar.

We have the same goals, but I am not sure we advocate taking the same paths or at the same time to reach those goals, but we are very pleased with the growing Canadian interest and activities in the field of disarmament. Furthermore, as you are aware, the Pugwash Conferences have on several occasions specifically endorsed the Canadian proposals for a technological freeze of the strategic nuclear arms race as presented by the Prime Minister to UNSSOD I and recently re-affirmed by him at UNSSOD II.

The Canadian Pugwash Group regards you as one of us. You have been with us in spirit for many years. We are grateful to you for having come; you arrived at only 1:30 this morning and you have to leave immediately on important government business. We appreciate your setting forth so clearly and in such detail what the Canadian Government's position is. This gives us the information we need to have in order to know better what we ought to be doing, and the ways we should be going forward, not only in our efforts to influence the Canadian Government, but also in our efforts to promote a saner and safer world.

All of us here are primarily interested in preventing a nuclear holocaust.

3. WAR CAN BE AVERTED:

A SOVIET PERSPECTIVE

Alexander N. Yakovlev

It is indeed both a pleasure and a privilege for me to be addressing this distinguished audience on the occasion of the 25th Anniversary of the Pugwash Movement. I am taking the floor here as a private person.

It is a significant moment for me to be able to speak from the same rostrum as many whose names have already become prominent in the text books of history.

Also I am especially delighted to see here Mrs. Eaton who continues the noble task of promoting the ideas worked out together with the late Mr. Eaton, ideas which have gained universal recognition. These ideas of peace and responsibility to all mankind, of cooperation between people, vividly show complete attachment to the cause which is at the very heart of our common human interest. This is the very heart which gives life to all hamanity, but which could also cease beating if mankind does not say to itself—enough is enough.

The Pugwash Movement stood at the very beginning of detente which brought such a great relief to all of us. And, in this lies its historical truth and importance.

The subject of this meeting—to discuss ways of saving humanity from nuclear incineration—is in my opinion of such importance that in dealing with it we must all try to overcome the differences of opinion between countries, parties, religions and political affiliation.

The choice facing us today is not what type of world each particular nation may choose, it is not a question of which values are better. The fundamental question for all mankind is whether we will choose to live together or die together.

This choice and risk is with us constantly, for no one can predict what will be the outcome of any explosive situation in the world, and there is no shortage of these in the world today.

Consciously or subconsciously we should not try to close our minds to this cruel and gruesome fact. There can be no happy end to the script so long as mankind is wasting over a billion and a half dollars a day on armaments.

The Soviet Union has viewed disarmament and arms control as a key aspect of its foreign policy, as the only reasonable alternative to a senseless and dangerous arms race, threatening to reduce our civilization to ashes, all of us. Nobody would look for a safe place in a snake's hole. And likewise nobody can safeguard peace by way of an arms race.

At the Second Special Session of the United Nations on Disarmament, the Soviet Union solemnly declared that it assumes the obligation not to be the first to use nuclear weapons. I am firmly convinced that this serious step opens important practical .possibilities for all those world leaders who are really interested in disarmament and in putting an end to the arms race madness.

In the search for measures which would actually halt the arms race, many political and public figures of various countries have recently turned to the idea of a freeze. This idea is close to the Soviet point of view.

We stand for limiting and eliminating nuclear weapons and are giving priority to nuclear disarmament. But we are also ready to negotiate controls and reductions of any weapon systems, naturally on the basis of equal security for each side.

We are not pessimists in the Soviet Union and we are confident that the present state of world affairs can and should be reversed, and that war can be averted. But peace is not a gift from the skies. In this connection, it is difficult to overestimate the role of contacts and meetings between representatives of various countries and in particular the prominent role of the Pugwash Movement which is providing a continuing means of communication and contact for scientists from all over the world.

In this connection, allow me to make a side remark. I was at the front during the Second World War at Leningrad. I believe all of you remember that terrible time. All of us in various degrees have enjoyed the post-war peace even though it was not always stable and quiet. This time of peace has convincingly shown that even the worst peace is better that the best war.

In the 50s, I was a post-graduate student at Columbia University where I studied various theories of international relations, reading Morgenthau, Warburg, Bowles, Kissinger's early writings, and other prominent American authors.

I disagreed with many assertions but I never doubted the validity of their arguments and their logic. Please bear in mind that my teachers were American professors—that is why I believe I have the right to make some modest assessments of some of today's concepts.

For example, the last three to four years I have been alarmed by concepts of punishment. You all know that it is not a new concept. But it is also well known that the practical use of that concept has never done any good. The Roman legionnaires destroyed Carthage and sprayed its soil with salt so that nothing could grow again on it, but this did not save the Roman empire.

During the Second World War, Nazis killed 20 million Soviet people, destroyed thousands of cities, factories, churches, declared all Slavic people inferior and doomed to extermination. All this was done under the pretext of "the Soviet threat". We were "punished" by rivers of blood and tears but it didn't save the Nazi empire from its crumbling.

After our revolution, Mr. Churchill made an appeal to "suffocate the Soviets in their cradle." I am reluctant to remind you what happened to the colonial empires after the Second World War, but it is a pleasure for me to remember that twenty years after these words of Churchill, we fought together. By recalling that, I just want to stress that history can play and sometimes does play its own game.

But it is not only historical experience which shows the senselessness and immorality of the use of punishments in international relations. The facts also confirm it. Only the arrogance of power prompts the idea of punishment—in fact it never happened that the weak and poor have declared sanctions against the powerful and rich. Besides, in my opinion, the concept of punishment creates and aggravates the atmosphere of distrust, hinders human contacts, brings about misunderstanding, irritation and suspicion. In other words, this concept when put into practice does not lead to any positive result. In my opinion, it is counter-productive from the point of view of the future cooperation of all nations.

Nobody is trying to find the feet of an eel or the wings of a turtle. The reason is simple—such things do not exist and they will not appear despite any claims of the theory of evolution. But already for thousands of years man has searched for his own reason, hoping for progress for future generations, and for the evolution of wisdom. Hope is the last thing that remains for man. Reason promotes hope and it would be terrible to lose hope and thus to lose faith in man's reason.

I am convinced that reason will prevail; it must prevail.

The great Aristotle said once that the only feature that distinguishes human beings from all other animals is an ability to blush. Let us try not to lose this human ability in the face of the difficult problems that may embarrass us.

Chairman:

I would like to thank the Soviet Ambassador to Canada for his brief and very perceptive statement. We appreciate your coming here from Ottawa and for giving us the benefit of your thoughts without our giving you an opportunity to prepare your remarks in advance. As you are aware, one of the aims of Pugwash is to promote human contacts and to bring about better communication and understanding between scientists of different nationalities and different political and social systems. I think your statement helps to promote those goals.

- 22 -

4. ARE THE SUPERPOWERS TO BLAME?

A SWEDISH PERSPECTIVE

Inga Thorsson

I am delighted and honoured to have been invited to participate in this 25th Anniversary Commemorative Meeting of the Pugwash Movement at its very birthplace. The history of this movement over the 25 years of its existence is a proud one. The work performed and the statements adopted by the various Pugwash Conferences have contributed very substantially to our fund of analysis and knowledge and to our awareness of the situation that we face in the nuclear age.

At no time in this age has it been more important than today to attain a combination of orderly scientific thinking and bold political leadership in order to deal with present dangers.

I believe that there exists ample evidence that orderly scientific thinking is available. What about bold political leadership? The tragic characteristic of the time in which we live is, of course, the singular lack of true leadership at top levels, political leaders with insight, imagination and initiative power to change, drastically, the present direction of international relations, particularly the arms race.

Nowhere has this fact been more apparent than in the United Nations General Assembly, at UNSSOD II which last Saturday concluded its five weeks of work with a less than a glorious final result. The main impression that these five weeks left on me, was that, once again, the leading forces, and especially the superpowers, have not shown themselves prepared to make use of the United Nations as an instrument for genuine disarmament efforts. The overwhelming majority of countries deplore this fact today. The leading military powers will themselves deplore it tomorrow.

Once again, the superpowers have shown themselves incapable of understanding the realities of the nuclear age. As James Reston of the *New York Times* remarked some time ago, *nobody*, now in charge of nuclear policy in the US, has ever seen a nuclear explosion. And they are singularly lacking in the imagination needed to grasp these realities. I should like all of them to go to Hiroshima, to stand humbly before the Peace Memorial Monument to read the words inscribed on it:

> "Let all the souls here rest in peace,
> for we shall not repeat the evil"

And let us draw the right conclusion: We must freeze the nuclear arms race. We must start the process of genuine nuclear disarmament. We must thus respond to requests from all over the world to stop this madness. For time is really running out, the nuclear threat increases with every lost year, with every lost opportunity.

In his most recent book, Nuclear Illusion and Reality, Lord Solly Zuckerman comes out forcefully for the need to focus immediately on achieving, at long last, a Comprehensive Nuclear Test Ban Treaty, as the decisive start of a nuclear disarmament process. There is no need for me to elaborate this—we all know the tragic history of the comprehensive test ban (CTB) negotiations. But there is every reason to recall its latest phase: the effort at UNSSOD II to get an agreed text on the compelling need to get multilateral CTB negotiations started. Although watered down to a bare minimum, the draft text was blocked by the United States and the United Kingdom.

This action will of course have to be judged against the background of the real US policy on the CTB, as outlined, for example, in a statement by Dr. Eugene Rostow, Director of the US Arms Control and Disarmament Agency, on 9 February this year in the Committee on Disarmament in Geneva. Although he stated, for which we should perhaps be grateful, that the *ultimate* desirability of a test ban has not been at issue, and that "a comprehensive ban on nuclear testing remains an element in the full range of *long-term* US arms control objectives," we should keep in mind that the US has joined repeated decisions, at the General Assembly in New York and in the Committee on Disarmament in Geneva, to accord to the CTB the highest priority of all items on the CD agenda.

But Dr. Rostow went on to say something even more stunning, and I quote him: "Limitations on testing must necessarily be considered within the broad range of nuclear issues." How can the lumping together of the CTB and "the broad range of nuclear issues" be in conformity with the legally binding commitments of the United States to a CTB Treaty (CTBT), as expressed in the second preambular paragraph of the partial test ban treaty of 1963, where parties pledged to seek the achievement of "discontinuance of all test explosions of nuclear weapons for all time," and as confirmed in the tenth preambular paragraph of the Non-Proliferations Treaty (NPT) of 1968?

There is nothing in these legally binding documents, that were signed and ratified by the US, that links the CTBT to "the broad range of nuclear issues." On the contrary, a CTBT is explicitly said to be sought on its own merits. The US has not abrogated these preambular paragraphs, nor made any announcements of its intention to interpret them in a new and less binding way. Is the US prepared to face a situation where it will be accused of a violation of legally binding international commitments?

The United States should weigh the practical political considerations related to its glaring refusal to accept full scope multilateral negotiations on a CTBT. This super-power should be aware of the rapidly mounting and fierce opposition among non-nuclear weapon states against the obstruction by the nuclear-weapon states to nuclear disarmament, particularly in the context of the NPT which calls for a cessation of the nuclear arms race, i.e. for vertical non-proliferation, in accordance with Article VI of that Treaty. What does the US think will happen at the third NPT Review Conference in 1985, three years from now, if by that time we do not have a multilaterally negotiated CTBT? Will that country, and its present Administration, take the risk of the collapse of the NPT, the only barrier that the international community possesses, however deficient, against horizontal nuclear weapon proliferation?

Questions of the same kind would have to be directed mainly to the United States concerning the other acute nuclear weapons issue at the UNSSOD II, the nuclear freeze. Sweden was together with, and at the initiative of, Mexico the sponsor of a draft resolution on that subject. We had of course no illusions about the outcome; it wasn't that consideration of the draft produced a negative result, there wasn't any consideration whatsoever. But the issue will come back at the 37th regular session of the General Assembly this autumn. What is important is, first that it will be one of the highly focussed issues in a number of States in the United States during the election campaign this autumn as a subject of a referendum, and that this is the result of a powerful popular movement for disarmament and peace at the grassroots level, and second that it represents a tremendous challenge to the United States to honour its own commitment to the NPT, Article VI of which prescribes negotiations in good faith, aimed at the cessation of the nuclear arms race at an early date and proceeding towards nuclear disarmament. That Treaty is 14 year old by now, it went into force 12 years ago. The commitment for a nuclear freeze "at an early date" is still not honoured. We shall continue to keep this issue on the official disarmament agenda. The future of humanity is at stake.

UNSSOD II is now behind us. I believe personally that, under the prevailing circumstances, no better result than the final concluding report could have been expected. The necessary prerequisites were simply not there to reach beyond the 1978 Final Document. And, again, the superpowers showed the same conspicuous lack of interest in the multilateral disarmament negotiations, as has been the case for years.

What will follow? Well, speaking to this distinguished audience of scientists, I have no revealing truths to announce. I can only give my views as a European politician, from one of Europe's few neutral countries.

What has happened—and not happened—so far in the field of disarmament negotiations in the nuclear age is to me evidence of the arrogance and the lack of insight and imagination of the nuclear-weapon states, particularly the superpowers, and their political leaders. The way in which they formulate their directives for on-going bilateral negotiations on issues, which concern the whole of humanity, is indeed an indication of this arrogant attitude. As a small piece of evidence, I read with some concern the text of the letter which President Reagan sent to General Rowny, the chairman of the US delegation to the START talks which opened on 29 June this year at Geneva. One sentence of the letter read: "As the two leading nuclear powers in the world, the US and the USSR are trustees for humanity in the great task of ending the menace of nuclear arsenals, and transforming them into instruments underwriting peace."

I want to say, in all sincerity, that the majority of the peoples of this earth entertain grave distrust of these two self-appointed "trustees for humanity." All states have the right to be equal partners for two reasons:

1. The nuclear-weapon states have shown themselves unable to free themselves from a situation characterized by a morally and politically insoluble dilemma.

2. All states, nuclear or non-nuclear, militarily aligned, neutral and non-aligned, share the common fate of a possible nuclear holocaust.

But instead of treating us as equal partners, the superpowers prefer secret bilateral talks behind closed doors, denying the multilateral Committee on Disarmament the right and the possibility of negotiating the highest priority items on its agenda. They disregard politically, although not legally, binding UN resolutions, on which they themselves have voted in favour. All this is part of their cynical and arrogant attitude towards the world around them.

One predominant reason for our present nuclear predicament is, as we all know, the trend in military research and development. This is currently moving in directions, which may well, unless checked within a decade, have rendered arms control, not to speak of disarmament, virtually impossible.

In turn this is closely linked with changing ideas on nuclear doctrines. Making, through research and development, nuclear weapon systems ever more accurate and rapid, the scientists and engineers force the strategists to rethink the way in which they would consider using politically and/or militarily, the might of nuclear power.

In undertaking this exercise, the strategists sometimes have recourse to arguments which clearly show the hollowness of the nuclear era. When, for instance, the doctrine of mutual assured destruction, MAD, came under attack a couple of years ago, it was said that it was not only militarily unacceptable, but also immoral.

I felt it difficult to follow the kind of argument used. If a particular nuclear doctrine is called immoral, but you don't want to give up your nuclear weapons, not even to proclaim a non-first-use policy, then another doctrine must be established that would be moral, or at least less immoral. The presupposition must be that you are prepared actually to use nuclear weapons in war, but are anxious to use them less immorally. So the flexible response and the counterforce doctrines were born. But these led to theories of "a limited nuclear war," which in turn developed into ideas of "a fightable and winnable nuclear war."

As a European, there is every reason for me to reflect on the effects of the prevailing mode of strategic thinking upon the countries in Europe—the smallest but one of the continents, the most densely populated, the most weapon-studded.

It has become obvious to everybody, that limited nuclear strikes will have widespread consequences and cannot stay limited. Therefore the whole doctrine of flexible response is encountering increasing public resistance. Ironically, recent attempts on both sides to further develop this doctrine by the deployment of new types of intermediate-range weapons is having the unexpected result to exposing the contradictory and impossible consequences of the whole doctrine—and, indeed, of nuclear weapons themselves.

The terrible dilemma of our present situation is, however, that it cannot be excluded, that in certain situations nuclear weapons would actually be put to their cataclysmic use—but the reply would of course be instant and equally cataclysmic. To ensure one's own defence, one would also ensure one's own utter and final destruction.

The need to rid Europe of this insane situation is obvious, but difficult to achieve. What has, almost lightheartedly, been implanted in and around Europe during the last three decades, cannot be removed overnight, without upsetting an established balance of terror, however precarious, and nefarious, it may be.

This, in my view, shows the hollowness of impossible and unacceptable nuclear doctrines, of the concept of deterrence and of the very possession of any nuclear weapons at all. This hollowness will become only more evident, as the arms race between the United States and the Soviet Union continues. There is no added security to be gained by anyone, through absurdly pursuing, in quantity and quality, the present arms race. There is only an ever increasing risk of a nuclear holocaust, destroying, not only human lives in the hundreds of millions, but also societal structure and the biological structure of this our only earth. This is the politically and morally insoluble dilemma shared by all the nuclear weapon states. This is the nuclear predicament, shared by all of us.

In this human predicament of the 1980's, are there any gleams of hope?

In my view, there is still no realistic basis for expecting any common sense from the political leadership of either of the superpowers. If there were, it would have shown us long ago. But there are, I think, two reasons for some hope.

One is, that both superpowers run the grave risk of letting their economies go to pieces, as, in times of serious economic difficulties, they continue a ruinous arms race. It is widely acknowledged that the true foundation of national security is a strong and healthy economy. It is difficult to escape the impression that the arms race is one of the major factors behind the prevailing economic crisis, spreading all over the world. A United Nations Governmental Expert Group, based on a mandate of the UN

General Assembly, and after three years of study, submitted last autumn a fairly voluminous report on the relationship between disarmament and development, which was to be discussed at UNSSOD II. The substantive consideration and the appropriate action requested by last autumn's Assembly did not, as we know, take place at UNSSOD II. But our analyses show convincingly the devastating effects on the economy of the way societies devote human and material resources to the arms race. Based on extensive research, we drew a number of conclusions which can be summarized in just two points; already quite widely quoted:

1) The world can either continue to pursue the arms race with characteristic vigour or move consciously towards a more sustainable international economic and political order. It cannot do both.

2) Irrespective of economic and social systems, irrespective of levels of economic development, there is a *mutual* and enlightened self-interest among *all* countries in effective disarmament.

Or, in the words of a strategic thinker of repute: The *economy* could become a factor for disarmament.

The *other* reason for hope is the sharply awakening public awareness of the tremendous risks that this generation and coming generations run if we allow the leaders of the world to continue their present course. For a growing number of people the issue has *changed*, from being one of *deterrence*, of *military* balance, of inferiority or superiority, into being an issue of survival. There is a rapidly increasing awareness of what a nuclear weapon actually is. For the first time since 1962, when Herman Kahn published his well known book, people are thinking about the unthinkable. One of the reasons is that they have suddenly understood that they will have to do so, because military and political leaders have made the unthinkable thinkable, i.e. by the logic of the nuclear doctrines, nuclear weapons are becoming *usable*. And this trend will have to be stopped.

The forceful and broadly-based peace movements in Western Europe and North America have already shown themselves to be important political factors influencing events. They are what George Kennan recently called the most striking phenomena of the early 1980's. They were to a high degree, present at UNSSOD II. Beyond that session they must continue to be so. There will have to be a worldwide constituency for disarmament, and it is there that the Pugwash Movement, because of its devotion and particular competence, will have to shoulder an increasingly important responsibility.

A brilliant Swedish author-performer-actor has written a musical fable called the Animal Congress, where the animals of the world try to save the human race from its own absurd foolishness, the arms race. The penguin cautions:

> When the meek are roused to anger
> let the arrogant beware.

Let the superpowers take heed.

Chairman:

After that devasting analysis of the terrible predicament of the world and of those who bear the main responsibility for it, there is little that can be added. Mrs. Thorsson, the Under-Secretary of State for disarmament of the Swedish Government, has long been admired as a forthright and courageous champion of disarmament. She and her country have certainly given leadership to the efforts to achieve disarmament and in particular nuclear disarmament. Her latest contribution was the outstanding report on the relationship between disarmament and development prepared for the United Nations by an international group of experts, of which she was the Chairman. That report, by itself, will be a lasting monument to her efforts. We thank you very much for your thought-provoking statement.

5. MANKIND MUST PROCEED TO DISARMAMENT
OR FACE ANNIHILATION

Alfonso Garcia Robles

In connection with my statement, Bill Epstein, with his usual kindness, told me that I could choose to speak for five minutes or for 25 minutes. I said I would take the five minutes and I think I have succeeded in doing so.

I consider it a privilege to participate in this celebration of the twenty-fifth anniversary of the Pugwash Movement which has rightly won the admiration and support of all peoples of good will. The reasons are many but on this solemn occasion I would like to mention only three:

Since its birth, the Pugwash Movement has always endeavoured to be a bridge between East and West; an effective instrument to build genuine detente and mutual understanding between nations with different economic and social systems.

Also since an early date it has become increasingly aware of the pressing need to find solutions which may contribute to improve substantially the unfair conditions of the Third World.

And last, but certainly not least, it has always been faithful to the letter and the spirit of the historic Russell-Einstein Manifesto, which had the foresight to state as early as 1955 that because of the discovery of nuclear weapons "we have to learn to think in a new way," adding further: "Here, then, is the problem which we present to you, stark and dreadful and inescapable: shall we put an end to the human race; or shall mankind renounce war?"

To appraise the visionary nature of such a pronouncement, we only need to recognize that it was almost a quarter of a century later that the United Nations General Assembly, in its Final Document of 1978—which Philip Noel-Baker has called "the greatest State paper in human history"—passed an essentially identical judgment when it declared:

Removing the threat of a world war—a nuclear war —is the most acute and urgent task of the present day. Mankind is confronted with a choice: we must halt the arms race and proceed to disarmament or face annihilation.

Let us hope that mankind chooses the first alternative of this decisive choice. And let the Pugwash Movement go on lending its full and unequivocal support to the achievement of this purpose.

Chairman:

My old and good friend Alfonso, former colleague in the UN Secretariat, later Foreign Minister of Mexico, father of the Treaty of Tlatelolco which established the only nuclear-free-zone in the world, and for some years Mexican representative at the Committee on Disarmament in Geneva, has outmaneuvred me. I didn't really believe that he would limit himself to five minutes. He has the reputation in the United Nations for eloquence and perception but not for brevity. Today he has also achieved the distinction of making the shortest statement at this commemorative session.

As many of you here know, he played a very important role in achieving the Final Document of UNSSOD. But I'll let you in on a secret that I don't believe anybody knows—the words he quoted from the Final Document were his own words.

He is also the father of the World Disarmament Campaign which was the only positive achievement at UNSSOD II.

It was no accident either that Inga Thorsson and Alfonso Garcia Robles were chosen this year as the first recipients of the Jo Pomerance Award as the two outstanding diplomats who had contributed most to disarmament.

6. THE PATH TO WORLD PEACE

Linus Pauling

For over 25 years the world has been in terrible danger—danger that a great nuclear war would take place, leading almost certainly to the extermination of the human race. Even though everyone knows that this danger exists, we have not been able to take action to decrease it and to regain control over militarism. Instead, we have made the systems of nuclear weapons and the vehicles of delivering them more and more complicated, and this growing complexity increases the chance that a technological or psychological error will occur that would initiate the catastrophic nuclear war that would probably bring to an end the era of intelligent beings on earth. I believe that the human race is going to survive, that our civilization will continue, that there will never be a Third World War in which nuclear weapons are used and our civilization is brought to an end. I believe that man's intelligence is going to overcome this great threat to its continuation, and I believe that the time to take action to achieve this goal is right now.

We all know that it is good for nations to end disputes by making treaties with one another, and that a few treaties about nuclear weapons and disarmament have been made. We have seen, however, that the process of moving toward disarmament and world cooperation by making treaties proceeds at an extremely slow pace. If the progress toward world peace is no faster in the future than it has been in the past, there is a high probability that the cataclysmic nuclear war will occur.

For many years I have advocated that progress toward control of nuclear weapons, achievement of world peace, general disarmament, and international cooperation be made by means of treaties, especially between the United States and the Soviet Union.

Let me quote from my book "No More War!", published in 1958.

I myself believe that it is possible for us to secure agreements with the Soviet Union to stop tests and to achieve disarmament and I believe further that the agreements could be of such a nature that the Soviet Union would adhere to them because it would be very much to her advantage to do so. . . . The time has now come for war to be abandoned, for diplomacy to move out of the 19th century into the real world of the 20th century, a world in which war and the threat of war no longer have a rightful place as the instrument of national policy. We must move toward a world governed by justice, by international law, and not by force. We must all, including the diplomats and national leaders, change our point of view. We must recognize that extreme nationalism is a thing of the past. The idea that it is just as important to do harm to other nations as to do good for your own nation must be given up. We must all begin to work for the world as a whole, for humanity.

Science is the search for the truth—it is not a game in which one tries to beat his opponents, to do harm to others. We need to have the spirit of science in international affairs, to make the conduct of international affairs the effort to find the right solution, the just solution of international problems, not the effort by each nation to get the better of other nations, to do harm to them when it is possible. . . . The time has now come for morality to take its proper place in the conduct of world affairs; the time has now come for the nations of the world to submit to the just regulation of their conduct by international law. . . .

If the world continues along the path of insanity, we are doomed to die—we Americans, all of us, and all the Russian people, and perhaps most of the people of European nations. Our civilization will come to its irrational end.

But I believe that we can prevent the great catastrophe. I believe that our government, with the support of the American people, can meet the challenge of the new crisis. I believe that we will abandon the mistaken policy of re-arming West Germany and Japan and will move forward vigorously, and with the cooperation of the Soviet Union and other nations, in achieving the solution of the terribly complex problem of safely reaching the goal of general and complete disarmament with control and inspection, and organizing the world community on principles of freedom and justice under law and mutual trust.

Twenty-four years have gone by, with little progress toward the goal. The process of moving toward disarmament and world cooperation by making treaties proceeds at an extremely slow pace. In fact, progress toward world peace by this route is so slow that I can say that it just does not take place.

I now believe that we can reach the goal by *unilateral action*—by a series of unilateral actions by the United States, the Soviet Union, and other countries, supplemented by international agreements as rapidly as they can be formulated and ratified.

I should like to see the United States take the lead in this process. The United States has been in the lead, ever since 1945, when we exploded our nuclear bombs over Hiroshima and Nagasaki. We have continued to be in the lead, although before long the situation has become such as to make it essentially meaningless to ask whether one nuclear power or the other was ahead in the power of destruction.

In fact, the United States has been taking unilateral actions throughout this entire period, but almost always in the wrong direction. Our representatives and those of the Soviet Union negotiated for seven years in order to formulate the SALT II treaty. We then took the unilateral action of refusing to ratify it—an action in the wrong direction. We introduced MIRV, and a few years later the Soviet Union was also equipping her rockets with multiple warheads. We are now considering an increase in the number of our nuclear weapons by 14,000. We have, unilaterally, developed the cruise missile. I do not need to quote all of the examples.

I think that the United States could now take unilateral actions that would greatly reduce the amount of military spending and at the same time increase the safety of the United States and of the rest of the world.

The way in which this could be done is discussed in detail in the book "The Price of Defense: A New Strategy for Military Spending," by the Boston Study Group—Randall Forsberg, Martin Moore-Ede, Philip Morrison, Phylis Morrison, George Sommaripa, and Paul F. Walker. One unilateral step toward disarmament could be taken by the United States, and we could call on the Soviet Union to take a similar step, and see whether or not the Soviet Union followed. I believe that the pressure on the Soviet Union to decrease the spending on armaments is greater than that on the United States, because the armaments expenditures represent a greater percentage of the wealth of the nation. Also, I am sure that the Soviet people and the Soviet government are more afraid of war than are the people and the government of the United States, because the Soviet people have experienced wars in a way that we have not.

The Boston Study Group advocates a decrease in the destructive power of nuclear weapons from the present completely insane level to a less irrational level, still great enough to serve as a deterrent to a Third World War. By their detailed analysis they showed that their policy would not only save tremendous amounts of money but would also greatly decrease the probability of world destruction.

Jerome Wiesner, in his essay of last month, began with the following paragraph.

There is an easily-structured, effective way to stop the escalating arms race. President Reagan should declare an open-ended unilateral moratorium, always subject to reversal, on the production, testing, and deployment of new nuclear weapons and delivery systems. He should invite the Russians to respond with a parallel declaration of purpose. If they did, it would result in a non-negotiated freeze. Only the President has the power and prestige to put this into effect; only he might have the courage to break such new ground and help reduce world-wide fear.... The challenge is to action, not negotiation. Once both countries have declared a moratorium, either can take the initiative to go further and further along the path. A moratorium, to be acceptable, must be safe for everyone—for us, the Soviet Union, and for both sides' allies. Is a moratorium safe? I believe that it is. . .

How long would it take to negotiate a "balanced" freeze? A unilateral moratorium is a safe way out of this dilemma. Ending the arms race with a moratorium means giving up attempts to match weapon for weapon and to achieve numerical balances among them, and depends instead entirely upon a secure deterrent. A moratorium does not have to mean "stop everything". . . . It is important to understand what a moratorium is, and especially, what it is not. It is not nuclear disarmament. It is a way of arresting the arms race. It is a unilateral path to a freeze. It can be ended at any time by a unilateral decision. What we ultimately do and how far we finally go beyond this easy initial state depends on how each side responds. The unilateral moratorium should be just a first step in global psychotherapy.

I believe that we can overcome the irrational drive toward race suicide.

I believe that human beings in the United States and the Soviet Union can cooperate to solve the great problems that we are faced with.

Nineteen years ago I said that "War and nationalism, together with economic exploitation, have been the great enemies of the individual human being. I believe that, with war abolished from the world, there will be improvement in the social, political, and economic systems in all nations, to the benefit of the whole of humanity."

I suggest that at this Pugwash meeting we consider issuing a manifesto, recommending that the great nations begin to take unilateral steps toward world peace and a rational future.

Well, can the Pugwash Movement make any significant contribution? I suggest that we stop the futile exercise of counting missiles, and warheads, and imagining irrational scenarios, and apply our intellect and influence to move the nations to take the unilateral actions that could save the world. There was a unilateral declaration by the Soviet Union: the statement that the Soviet Union would not be the first to use nuclear weapons. And the challenge to the United States to make a similar statement was rejected by the Government of the United States. I think we should apply pressure on the United States Government to make a similar statement and to follow it by some great unilateral step in the right direction.

Chairman:

I recall one unilateral action by Linus Pauling that, I was told by influential world statesmen, played a real role in achieving the first partial test ban treaty. He will remember, I'm sure, when he organized a petition and got some 1800 American scientists and some 13,000 scientists from around the world, including a large number of Nobel Laureates, to sign it. That petition called on the nuclear powers to "Stop Testing Now." I remember he brought that petition to Dag Hammerskjold at the United Nations. The impact of all of these scientists demanding an end to nuclear testing helped persuade the mothers of America and the public that it was time to insist on ending nuclear testing. It is an ideal way for scientists to use their expertise — to help inform and educate the public as well as governments.

It is a particular pleasure to have Linus Pauling with us. He is one of the two surviving signatories of the Russell-Einstein Manifesto. The last time I saw him was also on a 25th anniversary, when he came to New York for the 25th Anniversary of the United Nations. On that occasion he came as one of the living Nobel Peace Prize Laureates who presented to the United Nations an important Declaration on Peace and Disarmament that received great attention from the media.

I only want to add that Linus not only received a Nobel Prize for Peace but also one for Chemistry.

7. THE PURPOSE OF PUGWASH

Joseph Rotblat

Since we are commemorating the 25th anniversary of the first Pugwash Conference, I want to take you back 25 years and to speak about the first Pugwash. As it happened, I have been preparing the proceedings of the first Pugwash Conference, which were never published.

Since that First Pugwash, we have had 30 further conferences—three of them in Canada, the rest in other parts of the world and for each of them we have a volume of Proceedings.

The Pugwash Continuing Committee, which is now called the Pugwash Council, on several occasions resolved that we should produce these Proceedings of the first conference. The 25th anniversary of Pugwash provides the occasion to do so.

These proceedings are now being printed and will be available at the next Pugwash Conference in Warsaw next month, where the international Pugwash community will celebrate the 25th anniversary. And then the printed version will be sent to all other Pugwashites.

As you have heard, Pugwash started with the Russell-Einstein Manifesto which called on scientists to assemble in a conference to assess the danger to mankind from the new weapons of mass destruction and to <u>find means</u> to <u>avert</u> that danger.

That Manifesto was issued publicly by Bertrand Russell on the 7th of July at a large press conference in London. Within a few days after the proclamation Bertrand Russell received a letter from Cyrus Eaton offering hospitality to the proposed conference of scientists, including travelling expenses, and suggesting that this meeting be held in Pugwash. None of us had heard of a place called Pugwash.

Today, although Pugwash has not become a household word, there is no excuse for any intelligent person not to know about Pugwash. Pugwash now has an entry in the Oxford dictionary—in fact in the most popular edition, the Oxford Concise Dictionary. It is fairly well defined under, "Pugwash": "as in conferences—regularly held international conferences of eminent scientists to discuss world problems. As in Pugwash in Nova Scotia where first held."

Eventually we accepted Mr. Eaton's invitation and in July 1957, 22 of us from 10 countries assembled here in Pugwash. The program for the meeting consisted of three main topics:

- Radiation hazards from nuclear energy in war and peace

- The international control of nuclear weapons; and

- The social responsibility of scientists.

When I was preparing the volume of proceedings and rereading the papers, I found to my amazement that very little in the papers is really out of date, and most of it, in fact, is relevant to the present situation and could form the basis for Pugwash meetings in the future. Even if you take the most scientific point—the question of radiation hazards—I have to note that after two and one half decades of intensive research, there are still large uncertainties about the effects of exposure of man to radiation.

As for the consequence of an all-out nuclear war, this is now very hotly debated and is one of the main reasons for the new national and international physicians groups for social responsibility and for the prevention of nuclear war. Their analysis of the effects of nuclear war which are now widely discussed have had a deep impact on the public.

As for the international control of nuclear weapons, I think the number of steps which we have listed in the statement of the first conference are still as valid today as they were at that time. I want to read you just the last sentence, "The prompt suspension of nuclear bomb tests could be a good first step toward this purpose." After what we have heard this morning, I can see that we are still urgently in need of action on this first step.

Concerning the second responsibility of scientists, the points which were made then are certainly valid today— particularly when you recall that about half a million scientists and technologists, a very high proportion of the total, are engaged in military research. This is something which we, as a group of scientists, have certainly seen as a very challenging task before us.

The commemoration of an important event such as this is itself of course an important and valuable occasion. What we have heard this morning deals with the present situation, but it should also serve as a guide for the future and be based on what we have achieved in the past.

When we met 25 years ago we were all worried about the dangers to mankind of nuclear war, and some of us were convinced that nuclear war was imminent. We felt that we had to try to do something as scientists to prevent it. Well, 25 years after that event, we fortunately have had no nuclear war. While there's no way to apportion the credit, perhaps a tiny bit of that credit should go to Pugwash, largely on the basis of what was said this morning—that Pugwash established an independent informal channel of communication between the East and the West. This contributed to a certain extent to educating governments, and the public, and to making a nuclear war less likely.

Now, as we meet again, we are again a very worried group. The danger of nuclear war is still very large—some people would say it is greater than ever before. But still I feel that we should not despair. I think that if we can rekindle the spirit which helped us to start the first Pugwash, then I believe that we scientists can still make a contribution to the task of preventing a nuclear war for the next 25 years—and perhaps, even towards achieving our ultimate aim—securing lasting peace in this world.

Chairman:

We are all very happy to have Joe Rotblat here. He is here with dual credentials. Like Linus Pauling, he is one of the two living signatories of the Russell-Einstein Manifesto. In addition, he was one of the original 22 scientists present at the First Pugwash Conference here in Pugwash in 1957. In fact, although he isn't that old, he is the grand old man of Pugwash—he organized the Russell-Einstein Manifesto; he organized the First Pugwash; he was the first Secretary-General of Pugwash; he is still its guardian, watch dog, watchman and self-appointed historian.

One of the things that Pugwash did, as both Joe Rotblat and Linus Pauling will remember, was to invent something in 1962 that did not, and still do not, exist—the concept of "black boxes". They are automatic seismic stations, which were called "black boxes", which were to be set up as part of an international network to detect and identify seismic events or earthquakes, in order to distinguish them from underground nuclear tests. They are in the course of being set up in order to be able to verify a ban on underground tests and then make a comprehensive test ban treaty possible.

It is now 20 years since the idea was first proposed by Pugwash and a comprehensive test-ban treaty is still far away. The mills of the governments grind even more slowly than those of the gods when it comes to disarmament. Unfortunately they grind much more rapidly when it comes to producing armaments.

8. IF WE DO NOT ELIMINATE THE NUCLEAR THREAT

ALL OTHER PROBLEMS WILL BE IRRELEVANT

Theodore M. Hesburgh

At a time when not many people in the world were listening to what Bertrand Russell and Albert Einstein and their associates had to say about the necessity of peaceful solutions to world problems in a newly nuclear world, the Pugwash Movement led the way. Through the cold war, Pugwash brought great scientists and scholars from both sides together to forge new links of understanding and common resolve across a thermonuclear chasm. During detente, the Pugwash Movement built on the foundations it had constructed during the cold war period. Now, at a new period of confrontation and denunciation, Pugwash's voice of reason is still heard, especially during this twenty-fifth anniversary year.

I can bring only one small voice and perhaps one unique message to this assembly. If I do so in autobiographical fashion, I trust you will forgive me, for there is no other way I can tell my story.

A little more than a year ago, a friend of mine, an officer of the National Academy of Sciences in Washington, D.C., called me about one of his concerns. He said that at a recent meeting of the International Council of Scientific Unions, it became apparent that there was unanimous support for the removal of the nuclear threat to humanity. The same was true of our own Academy of Sciences and probably of most Academies in the world. However, despite quasi-unanimous resolutions from scientific bodies everywhere, nothing seemed to be happening among political leaders, and all too little (at that time) among the public at large. His query to me: Is there not some way of bringing together, possibly for the first time since Galileo, the scientific and the religious leaders of the world who are opposed to nuclear war?

As a Roman Catholic priest, I thought first of my own religion of three quarter of a billion members worldwide and a very articulate Pope. For fifteen years, from 1956 to 1971, I had represented the Vatican at the International Atomic Energy Agency in Vienna. There I had associated with Franz Cardinal König who spoke of the peaceful uses of atomic energy at an annual Mass in the Stephansdom for all of the delegates to the General Conference. He was later associated with meetings of Nobel Laureates in Europe and developed a special interest in the relationships of science and religion.

As a first response to my Academy friend's question, I invited Cardinal König to visit America and arranged for him to meet concerned people in New York, Washington (at the Academy), Chicago, San Francisco, Los Angeles, and Dallas. It was obvious to him from this trip that there was great concern for the nuclear threat to humanity, especially in the scientific community.

A few weeks later on November 11th, 1981, there was an all-day teach-in at over 150 United States universities. I think every university, like our own, had twice as many students turn up as had anticipated. I offered Mass for the faculty and students and preached on the morality or immorality of nuclear war. Following this, one of our alumni, Dr. James Muller of Harvard, Secretary of the Physicians for Social Responsibility, spoke on the medical effects of a one magaton bomb exploded over a large city. The picture was devasting. As I walked back to my office, I experienced something almost like a religious conversion. For thirty years, I have been deeply engaged in trying to create a better world, in the face of the extreme poverty in Asia, Africa, and Latin America, working to alleviate world hunger, to oppose the denial of human rights at home and abroad, working against tropical diseases afflicting hundreds of millions of humans, against illiteracy and for education—and suddenly it dawned on me—if we do not eliminate the nuclear threat, all of these other problems will be irrelevant, for there will be no more humans on earth to have problems, or if a few do survive a probable nuclear holocaust, their problems will be those of the Stone Age.

As a result of this newborn conviction, I decided to redirect most of my worldwide efforts to one immediate effort: to bring prominent scientists and prominent religious leaders together worldwide to denounce the nuclear threat and to promote specific steps to eliminate it.

Six months and six trips abroad later, I can report today that we are will on our way to accomplishing this. Cardinal König and I met in Vienna during three days of February, this year, with the Presidents of the Science Academies of Japan, India, France, England, and the Pope's Pontificial Academy of Sciences. We also had with us the Vice President and Foreign Secretary of the Russian Academy, the Representative of the President and Foreign Secretary and other members of the United States Academy, a distinguished German physicist as well—eight nations in all. The Chinese delegates invited could not come at that time, but expressed interest in future meetings.

Following three days of discussion and unanimous agreement in Vienna regarding the dimensions, the context, and the step-by-step possible solutions to the nuclear threat to humanity, four more meetings were planned for the immediate six months ahead. Two are already completed. A statement of our Vienna consensus was elaborated at the Royal Society in London by USSR, US, UK, French, and Indian scientists. The draft was then discussed and approved at a meeting of these scientists with members of the Pontifical Academy in Rome in June. The draft was then sent to the heads of some fifteen National Academies —including all the nuclear powers, who will meet with Pontifical Academy members to discuss, possibly amend, and then present the statement to Pope John Paul II in Rome in September.

Following that, Cardinal König and I hope to meet during October in Vienna with all of the world religious leaders we can bring together there, and also with scientists involved in this endeavor.

Religious leaders are almost always accused of being naive when passing moral judgments on as complicated a matter as nuclear war. This time, they come armed wih the best information that the scientific community can provide. Together, they form a powerful alliance. The religious leaders can raise the consciousness of billions of their religious constituencies, Muslims and Jews, Hindus and Buddhists, Confucianists and Christians.

The ultimate solution to this problem is, of course, political. My hope is that once the universities, their students and faculties united, the physicians, the artists, the writers, the journalists, and the worldwide scientific and religious leadership join voices and make common cause against the nuclear threat to humanity, the politicians will have to listen and to act or they will find themselves suddenly replaced by those who will listen and act.

The hour is late. Only by working together can humans of all nationalities save our common humanity.

I need not tell this group that the hour is late. I think only by working together in the Pugwash tradition can humans of all nationalities serve our common humanity.

I think Einstein said that the advent of nuclear weapons changed everything except the way people thought about the world. That is the most important and most needed change of all.

Chairman:

"Father Ted", as everybody knows the Reverend Theodore Hesburgh, has certainly demonstrated that he is a true Pugwashite in spirit. He is of course familiar to all of us as the President of Notre Dame University. Beyond that he is known throughout the length and breadth of this land and, indeed, throughout the world as a great promoter of peace and human survival. His brilliant idea of marrying scientific and religious leaders in the struggle to eliminate the nuclear threat to humanity certainly conforms with the concept and activities of Pugwash. We wish him great success in that great task. And we are grateful to him for finding the time to fit us into his busy schedule.

9. SOME REMINISCENCES OF

THE FIRST PUGWASH MEETING

Iwao Ogawa

I participated in the historical first Pugwash Conference as a young assistant to the late Professor Hideki Yukawa, my uncle, and also to the late Professor Sin-itiro Tomonaga.

In the first Conference here, I joined the so-called "Committee One" on radiation hazards convened by Professor Rotblat, together with Professor Tomonaga, and worked hard to compare our own fallout data in Japan with those obtained in other countries. Since I was perhaps the only nuclear physicist who was exposed to the flash and the blast of the first atomic bomb dropped on Hiroshima, I had naturally been strongly interested in the nuclear weapons problem and was devoting myself to the study of the effects of fallout radiation in our laboratory.

In the Committee, we considered many problems that were all key issues at that time so that the discussions were quite heated and continued often until very late in the evening. Very often I could hardly follow the quick English spoken by English-speaking members like Professor Muller, Dr. Selove and Professor Rotblat and I wondered if the debate was becoming a serious quarrel, particularly when Professor Muller suddenly stood up from the chair and talked in a violent tone and with sharp penetrating eyes while walking round and round in the small room. Were it not for the relieving smile of Professor Muller at the end of each statement, I might have been unable to stand the unusually keen tension which prevailed there.

As a result of much hard work, many problems were adequately resolved and we completed a concise but valuable report. The contents of the report were remarkable in many respects. For example:

1) The report clarified for the first time the global character of the fallout from nuclear tests and hence from a possible nuclear war.

2) The fact that there was practically complete agreement in the fallout data from various countries was in itself a remarkable new finding. This was the more remarkable because the agreement was reached between scientists from the opposing East-West blocks and from nuclear and non-nuclear countries, as well as from Japan which was unique in its suffering from radiation hazards.

3) An appropriate and adequate evaluation was made of the supposed linear relationship between the dose of radiation on incidence of leukemia and other somatic effects of radiation, and a logical method was established for the first time for estimating the number of possible victims of nuclear tests and of any possible nuclear war.

My strong impression there was that scientists can sometimes fulfill their social responsibility by pursuing their own work as experts, and by making this type of assessment which nobody else can do.

Furthermore, I was greatly enlightened and interested in the more political discussion by many participants about how to achieve arms control and nuclear disarmament.

In particular, I cannot forget the unique proposal of Professor Szilard for minimum nuclear deterrence as a tentative method of avoiding the imminent danger of nuclear war.

More than that, I was greatly moved by his talk at an informal meeting in the Thinker's Lodge one evening prior to the formal session. He told us in a grave tone how he and his colleagues in the Manhattan Project had made efforts but eventually had failed to stop the direct use of atomic bombs on Japanese cities. His sincere sentiments of deep regret greatly helped the Japanese participants who had feared that American scientists might be more arrogant or lack reflective thoughtfulness about the matter.

The greatest feature of the first conference was, I think, that all the participants there were very friendly to each other and shared a common concern about the threat of nuclear weapons endangering human survival.

It is 25 years since then, and nuclear weapons are still accumulating at an even greater rate in spite of the constant and relentless efforts of the Pugwash Movement, also in spite of the recent growth of a public mass movement for peace and disarmament. Our common enemy, the nuclear weapon, appears to be still very strong and formidable.

Here I recall a very funny but meaningful joke which professor Szilard told us. The joke was something like this:

> There was a very pious lady who had never had a word of blame for anybody. A cruel man heard of this and asked her: "What do you think about the Devil?"
>
> She thought for a while, and then answered him, calmly and with a smile: "He is very diligent. He works very hard night and day."

As Professor Szilard pointed out, the devil in man always drives him on. It drives him to stick with nuclear weapons. How to overcome this is still the main task of our Pugwash Movement.

Chairman:

We are all happy to welcome back to Pugwash the youngest participant in the first Pugwash Conference and the only Pugwashite that I know who was present in Hiroshima when the atom bomb was exploded there. It is somewhat ironic that at the First Pugwash they were discussing minimum nuclear deterence, whereas now every unnecessary new spiral in the race to overkill and oblivion is justified on the phony ground that it is needed to improve deterrence. The world seems really to be going from MAD to NUTS, from Mutual Assured Destruction to Nuclear Utilization Target Selection.

10. MORE OPENNESS:

AN INTERNATIONAL

SATELLITE SURVEILLANCE SYSTEM

Sir Mark Oliphant

First, let me mention the great feeling of nostalgia that the original participants feel in returning to the little village of Pugwash because it all began here and has become part of our lives and a living Movement throughout the world. Joe Rotblat and Cyrus Eaton, and now Mrs. Cyrus Eaton, have made a great contribution in launching and nurturing the Pugwash movement.

The world is in a technological mess at the moment—arising from the unprecedented rate of increase in natural knowledge, which we call science, and its application in technology. And I don't believe that *words* are any answer to the problems created by technology. There have been too many of them. Over the last 25 years, or more than that, through the lifetime of the old League of Nations and then of the United Nations, we have had words and words and words about disarmament, and nothing has happened. I think it is time that we tried to take some practical actions.

At the early Pugwash meetings, we did discuss hardware—as it were—and experiments that could be made to get the information which would facilitate some logical practical approach to disarmament—particularly nuclear disarmament. But that seems to have faded out, as it has in the United Nations in favor of more and more words.

Words do *not* produce an answer, unless they are followed up by practical action. As has been pointed out, the words uttered today about the question of nuclear war and human survival are only echoes of statements made long ago. The same sentiments, and almost the same sentences are used. In terms of action, nothing has been

achieved.   Even today, I have heard nothing that is
new—so far.

I believe that there may be a technological answer to
this problem that we face, if it is pursued with a small
percentage of the effort that is devoted to the arms race,
which is of course an enormous technological investment.
But it must be undertaken not by the great powers, but by
those who now feel impotent in the face of the arrogant
assumption of leadership in all things—in war, in social
responsibility, in economic clout—which is made by the
great powers. The basic problem, expressed years ago by
the gentle Niels Bohr, is lack of openness and the resulting
generation, by secrecy, of fear and suspicion.   If there
were no secrecy, the possibility of war might disappear
completely.   Preparations for war—actual war activities
—depend entirely on secrecy, on the other chap not
knowing what you are doing.

Technological spying—provided the results are made
public and available to all—might therefore eliminate
secrecy.   Neither of the great powers could do this—
except when it might be to their own military or economic
advantage, it just isn't possible for them to undertake such
a thing in the present state of tension in the world.
America and Russia regard Europe as expendable in their
own defence, although it is the cradle of our civilization.
But the nations of Europe, together with the other technologically advanced nations—which are individually small
and impotent—both in the eyes of the great powers, and
unfortunately in their own estimation—possess all the
technical ability to develop technological spying to the
stage where no nation can any longer possess military or
economic secrets of any importance.   For instance, it is
the aircraft blind landing system developed in my own
insignificant country, Australia, Interscan, which is now
being adopted universally throughout the world for control-
ling the blind landing of aircraft.   And there, in competition with the giants, a tiny little nation had some people
who had ideas which were original and practical. So we are
not without the ability to do these things.

I propose that surveillance by satellite, and every other
optical and electronic means, replace the participation in

the arms race which is forced upon them by their great allies. Using the growing techniques for integration of information, including holography and sideways-looking radar, satellite surveillance could detect rabbits on the ground. This is what I'm told by the experts at the present time. The resolution can be increased enormously by using two or more widely separated satellites in isochronous order as with long-base-line astronomical observations. Several sophistocated satellites could be made and launched for the cost of one aircraft. Without great financial strain, all the satellites required for these purposes could be provided and operated by the smaller nations and the results released to the whole world—without consultation with, without any approval from, and without any kowtowing to either of the superpowers.

I believe myself that countries like Canada, the European nations, and other nations throughout the world that are reasonably sophisticated from the point of technology could undertake such a task which would so force on all nations Niels Bohr's concept of openness, that war and the arms race would come to have no significance or value to anybody, and would then cease—just from atrophy—just from the fact that they were useless.

I do hope that in our discussion we will have some mention of practical action that might arise from Pugwash meetings as they did from the very early ones which were very helpful in doing away with atmospheric testing and other ways.

Chairman:

Sir Mark Oliphant was the participant who came furthest —all the way from Australia—both for the First Pugwash Conference and for this commemorative meeting. We are delighted that he could come, particularly since his statement is in the true Pugwash tradition. More openness in world affairs has always been a Pugwash aim, if not always emphasized as much as it should be. And it was at the Pugwash Conference at Mühlhausen in 1978, where Abe Chayes, Ted Taylor and I presented a proposal for an

- 55 -

international surveillance satellite for all. The proposal was commended as worthy of study by Pugwash, and it was published in *The Bulletin of the Atomic Scientists.* Later it was picked up by the French Government and presented by the President of France to the UN at the First Special Session on Disarmament. The idea is being actively pursued by France and a number of other countries, although without any support from the two superpowers. The French Pugwash Group has held one international symposium on the subject two years ago and will convene another one later this year. Hence, Sir Mark, there are some hopes that the idea will become a reality. I agree with you that Pugwash might push the idea more than it has.

11. LEARNING TO THINK IN A NEW WAY

Sergei Kapitza

It is a great honor to be here at this meeting commemorating the first Pugwash event that started a new pattern of meetings of scientists concerned with world affairs. I belong to the second generation of Pugwashites, and I would like here for a moment to remember some of my compatriots who were here, and alas, will never be with us anymore. Academician A.V. Topchiev was the first to come here to this place, and was the first to help this dialogue get started. Then we have Academicians M.P. Millionshchikov and L.A. Artsimovich, the man who conceived the "black box" which concept can be applied to many of the issues facing us—a concept that is still useful. I bring a message of best wishes from Academician M.A. Markov and V.C. Emelyanov of the Soviet Pugwash Group, and from my father, Peter Kapitza.

Today I would like to talk about what has really happened, and maybe try to think what can happen next. I do hope that this movement will survive and will flourish in the future. Of course, if we refer to the Russell-Einstein Manifesto which provided the basis for these discussions, its main message was to learn to think in a new way about the new weapons of the new nuclear technology.

The first meetings took place in private. They were attended mainly by natural scientists, with no diplomats, and no press. Perhaps that is why some people thought that fewer words were produced than is the case nowadays.

But these important dialogues led to the concept of practical detente, to coexistence, to ways of understanding that fighting can no longer be a way of settling the issues facing the world. I think an important dialogue has really developed between those who are politicians and know the art of the possible, and the scientists, who with a certain arrogance, think that they know the art of the impossible. This was a bridge which has had to be built.

The world has lived in relative peace for more than 30 years. That we have managed to live in nuclear peace for that period is in a great measure a tribute to those who relentlessly fought against the nuclear menace in these years. It is all the more important that we do not relax our efforts in combatting those who strive to make nuclear war acceptable, to condition people to its use.

Not only do we have to prevent the outbreak of nuclear war, we also have to find ways of resolving the differences facing us all. Speaking now from the Soviet point of view, I think we cannot in all cases share the responsibility for what is happening in our divided world. But I think I am expressing the spirit of our leaders when I say that we are ready to discuss any and all of those issues and, through discussion, to find ways of resolving the difficulties that face us all.

Today I would like to speak as a scientist, not as a specialist on disarmament and arms control. Also, I have some experience in presenting science to the general public. Sometimes it is asked whether Pugwash should go public or not. I would not put it in this extreme way. I think the machinery for our deliberations, the Working Groups that have been established, as well as the spirit that has been generated are important, and should be kept as they are. But the messages that we manage to develop need to be published and to be publicized.

What should be our next step—for the next 25 years, to the close of this century? This whole millennium of world history has been wracked with struggle and conflict and war. Can we change this pattern? What has really happened now is that a new generation has emerged which in most countries has never experienced war. I think it is very proper to ask what Pugwash can do in the fateful years which are ahead. We really live in a period of change, a period that a physicist would describe as a phase transition when things happen. Order or disorder may appear.

We have all witnessed the growth of potential differences that in the past have led to world wars. These are the global issues of resources, population expressed in the pressure of space, and economic differences in our divided world. These changes are rapid and happen in many dimensions. We also see that grave difficulties in economic development have generally emerged. The economic machinery that in different societies had led in the past to progress has now in many places lost its former efficiency.

Finally, new global problems have been recognized. Today the development of these major socio-scientific issues hopefully paves the way for a new way of thinking. What we have really been doing here is discussing the global problem of disarmament—it is a global problem, and it can be classified as such.

What really matters for dealing with global problems, above all other considerations, is the development of a new mentality; and this is the factor that has taken the longest and is hardest to develop. Those people who were responsible for the invention of the atomic weapon recognized, after a few years, the menace of this weapon to mankind, but it took 25 years to get that message across to the people—fortunately without the experience of a nuclear war. But that is the difference in time scale which exists between the time needed to invent a new device and the time it takes to develop a responsible attitude toward it. This is a time lag that seems to be inherent in human nature.

The same thing has happened with the motor car, with television, with the computer, and with atomic energy. The society which creates these things and is in turn shaped by them finds it extremely complicated to take an objective and responsible position towards them.

A caustic wit once described the United Nations as a most expensive educational institution. What is Pugwash, if not a similar device? However, it is not so expensive— perhaps owing to its exclusive nature. To what end must we apply the very special talent assembled here, and toward what goal should we direct ourselves in the future? Our founding fathers pointed out the dangers of a nuclear war, and, in singling out this most important issue, they gave us an example of how our efforts should be directed.

Nuclear weapons lead to universal oblivion; this fortunately has been recognized. But is it not our duty, the duty of scientists to seek a way to instill hope in the next generation. Today I must say that worldwide—especially in the advanced nations—we witness various symptoms of disillusion with science, if not outspoken distrust. Is this a reaction to the absence of a human message in science? Is science running out of whatever moral credit it has? Or is this disaffection a sign of a certain childhood disease that will pass in time and even provide some sort of immunity to irrationalism? Or are we witnessing the signs of a deeply-lying crisis of confidence in science and human reason?

As has been repeatedly said but not yet acted upon, we have to learn to think in a new way and not turn away from this challenge. That a more human approach in matters of nuclear weapons is necessary has been very powerfully illustrated by the way the message of doctors on the nuclear threat was received and the reaction that was generated. Perhaps the seed had been planted many years before, and it took the doctors to give it the final stimulus that led to the worldwide reaction that we now witness. I think that not only statesmen, but natural scientists have a lesson to learn here. Recently in Moscow we had a very interesting television broadcast by six doctors. Four thousand doctors had come to Moscow to discuss heart disease at a conference on cardiology. Three American and three Russian doctors headed by Academician Chazov, a very well-known cardiologist and a man of great responsibility in our medical world, for more than an hour, discussed in an outspoken manner in English and Russian, to an audience of more than 60 million people, the nuclear issues that are facing us in the stark and sensible language of professional doctors. It was an extraordinary performance. It appeared at 6 p.m. on a Saturday on Russian television after having been announced the day before in a two minute news flash during the main national news program. It was a most important message for the people of our country. Many questions were posed, and it will take a long time to finish answering all the questions raised. In fact I have tapes of that broadcast with me, and perhaps we could find some time to use them here.

Perhaps today it would be well to remember that of all the conflicts in the modern world, there is still one more—that is the problem of man and the world tensions which he himself has created. When we start discussing these global problems, to many they seem remote, not human in their scope and scale or content. In discussing the increasing carbon dioxide in the atmosphere, people ask what this implies, does it mean one should not have a motorcar, or what? The message and content of these global issues affect the behavior, and need the understanding, of everyone. It is not easy to deal with these global issues, but it has to be done if we are to develop the mentality of thinking in a new way. On the other hand we cannot do that unless more consideration is given to people's human concerns. Perhaps that is one of the lessons that we also have to learn from the doctors who certainly do know how to deal with human beings.

It is really the human condition that is the final aim of all our efforts—to create a way of life in dignity and freedom. Are not these the main social changes, the most important ones in the world of the future—where the broadest ideas of socialism in treating global issues are to be combined to serve the happiness of man himself?

These global problems, and those of mankind, are interdisciplinary ones and they demand a new approach, a new way of thinking in which we have to transcend the divisions of scientific discipline.

In our highly specialized and diversified world of learning, this is not an easy thing to do. Perhaps here the organizational framework can be of some help. In the Soviet Union, it was felt some time ago that it would be useful to establish a coordinating body, a clearing house for information and expertise in matters of peace and disarmament. For this a Council on problems of peace and disarmament was set up. It operates under the aegis of the Academy of Sciences and the State Committee for Science and Technology of our government. It has various sections headed by Arbatov, Gvishiani, and Markov, whose names are familiar to you. The chairman of this committee is Academician N. Inozematzev, and it is housed at the Institute for International Relations and World Economy. I think it is a sensible thing—not in order to give guidance to all the efforts that are taking place, but to bring them under a common umbrella and to somehow unite their efforts in an interdisciplinary effort.

I think there are certain lessons here that may be useful to others. I can even envisage a network of such institutions which could help develop a new mentality to integrate and use the findings and thinking of scientists concerned with human issues.

Then we have also to explore improved ways to deliver our message. Here much can be done to communicate, once an appropriate intellectual message exists. The mass media can be very powerful, especially television which acts persuasively, incessantly, and has an enormous effect on human society.

It is the duty of all of us present to recognize the need for a scientific approach to the problems of humanity. It is only thus that we can properly choose our path and find a way to instill hope—not only through the renunciation of nuclear weapons as the main menace to our future, but also by generating new ideas, exploring new approaches and finding new paths. Here we require vision and imagination.

A man at 25 is supposed to be in full command of his faculties. It is also said that a scientist becomes great by choosing the proper problem. Pugwash is clearly in full command of its faculties, and the problems chosen are certainly worthy of our full attention.

Chairman:

We are all indebted to Sergei Kapitza for that thoughtful statement and to the Soviet Pugwash Group for having chosen him to participate in this commemorative meeting. He has given us some new insights into Einstein's edict that we must learn to think in a new way, and he has done so with eloquence and elegance.

12. WHERE WE OUGHT TO BE GOING

Bernard T. Feld

I want to say a few words today about where I think we ought to be going. The immediate goals of Pugwash are clear. If you look around the world today the obscenely large piles of nuclear weapons in the hands of the superpowers are something that threatens us all. It is obvious that something will just have to be done to start to reduce and eventually to eliminate them.

It has been pointed out by a number of people that if the nuclear stockpiles of either the United States or the Soviet Union, or both, in any combination whatsoever, were reduced by 50 percent tomorrow, nobody would know the difference. It would not make the slightest difference whatsoever in the ability of either or both of the two nations to act in any sphere in which they are interested in acting, and in fact, it would not make the slightest difference in the ability of either side to deter attacks by the other. Furthermore, if that 50 percent were 70 percent, it would still not make any difference—although people might start to take notice.

Consequently there is a tremendous amount of room for purely unilateral activity on the part of our leaders. I feel really rather annoyed and ashamed, that, although a number of such steps have recently been taken by Premier Brezhnev of the Soviet Union, this has apparently just gone completely unnoticed—or at least unremarked upon by the news media in the West. The unilateral declaration of no-first-use on the part of the Soviet Union is to my mind a very significant step. The proposal for the unilateral freezing of nuclear forces in Europe, the reduction—if not by a large amount, at least by a certain measurable number—of the SS-20s targeted on Europe and of other older, perhaps more obsolete SS-4s and SS-5s has gone unremarked, unnoticed and unreciprocated. A number of us have for many years felt that what was needed was for some unilateral step to be taken by one of the sides, which would undoubtedly be followed by some sort of reciprocated action on the part of the other. Apparently, the problem is more complicated and not as automatic as that. The first unilateral action or proposal has to be noticed, or at least noticed sufficiently, so that our leaders are forced to take account of them.

But something *is* going on. The recent statements of American leaders announcing their willingness to engage in discussions of arms control, at least in the European theater, is a direct consequence of the pressures which have been placed on our government. These pressures come in large part from the European public which is threatening now to take the issue into its own hands and to denuclearize Europe without agreement, if agreement is not forthcoming. I think these kinds of pressures are extremely important. Certainly Pugwash ought to be in the forefront. It should examine specifically how the scientific community can contribute to these increasing pressures on our Government.

In addition, I think that Pugwash should undertake more seriously a task which it performed very effectively in its early days—that is, to make proposals and to start to think out how one can get them onto the negotiating table of arms control and arms reduction. We must pursue the limitation, not only of the growth of arms, but also of the even more dangerous explosive growth of arms technology and particularly of the new technologies for the use of nuclear arms and delivery systems. I think we have a long way to go in this direction. I think we need to think through how we can in fact get this process moving at a time when the levels on both sides are so obscenely high. Yet each side is afraid to make even a small meaningless move for fear that somehow or other it will lose something—although it is difficult to see what it is that it might lose.

I think we have a very important role to play in demystifying the concept of verification that seems to engulf every new proposal before it is even made. I think if one really studies the verification problem, it is a minor problem for any arms control measure that might be of interest. If the United States or the Soviet Union were to reduce long range delivery systems by 50 percent, there would be no verification problem. And who would care if the 50 percent turned out to be 55 percent or 45 percent for that matter? It wouldn't make the slightest difference. One doesn't have to see every last military action in the Soviet Union to have a very good idea of what is going on with respect to the deployment of nuclear weapons. National reconnaissance methods provide very extensive information.

I think we really have to understand the minor role of verification and that it is used as a device for permitting nations to refuse to do what they did not want to do in the first place. We must seek to overcome the internal political problems, which requires an understanding of what these political problems are. However, we must not be carried away by the technical difficulties.

Even more, I believe we must start to be very imaginative in thinking of schemes where science and technology can be used in a cooperative rather than a competitive fashion to solve some of these problems. Sir Mark Oliphant has mentioned a number of useful programs that can be undertaken on both sides to use technology to help to make more stable the kinds of fairly drastic arms control arrangements which would be possible and necessary.

We could think of going further. For example, we could reexamine the notion that there must be two parallel, completely independent programs for the exploration of the planets and outer space—one by the Soviet Union and its allies, and the other by the Western nations, in which both sides are doing essentially the same thing in full view of the other. Many of these competing programs do not have any serious military applications in spite of the propagandistic effort of people who find it convenient to talk about military implications merely to raise money to do things which they would like to do anyhow. In a field that has so many interesting new discoveries, inventions, and new technologies to present to the human species, to have two parallel, independent programs going on is the height of stupidity. Thus, we should try to achieve very rapidly an agreement on space applications and space exploration which is similar to the agreement on the exploration of the Antarctic which has been in effect now for more than 20 years. The cooperative efforts undertaken under this agreement has limited, but in some ways important, scientific interest.

Projects of this kind, where mutual cooperation is obviously to the benefit of both sides, irrespective of what else we do in the world, are things we should be seeking out and developing and which we should be presenting in a very serious fashion for the scientific communities of all the nations concerned.

Pugwash does have a program. Our main program relates to convincing our colleagues, our peoples and our governments of the feasibility and importance of arms reductions, and of arms control. We also have the very positive aim of devising and spelling out programs of cooperation which will lead both the United States and the Soviet Union into the 21st Century with greater vested interests in further cooperation than our present vested interests in competition.

Chairman:

Bernie Feld, surprisingly, was not a participant in the First Pugwash Conference. Nonetheless, next to Joe Rotblat, he most personifies Pugwash, and not only the American Pugwash Group. He should have been at the First Pugwash since he worked with Leo Szilard, and he also was involved in the making of the atomic bomb. I should say in his defence— which he of course does not need and which he himself sometimes says—he has been atoning for it ever since. He drives himself mercilessly. Among his many activities is that of Editor-in-Chief of the Bulletin of Atomic Scientists. Bernie succeeded Joe Rotblat as Secretary-General of Pugwash and is now Chairman of the Executive Committee of Pugwash. The normal condition of the US Pugwash Group, unlike the Canadian Group of course, is one of complete disarray. But whenever you need to communicate with the somewhat mythical American group, Bernie is always there.

Bernie is also a wonderful person to work with. We were co-chairmen and co-editors of the book on the Pugwash Symposium on "New Directions in Disarmament." Bernie was very cooperative. He let me do all the work and all the writing—but he agreed instantly with all my suggestions, which greatly improved the efficiency of the operation! But I must admit his advice and experience are invaluable.

13. AMERICAN ATTITUDES TO ARMS CONTROL

James Leonard

I was surprised yesterday evening when I learned that I would have the opportunity to contribute a few remarks. I was also quite puzzled. What could I possibly add to the observations made by such distinguished fellow Americans as Dr. Pauling, Father Hesburgh, and Dr. Feld? On reflection, I concluded that Bill Epstein had put me on the program out of a belief that the most convincing, the most impressive testimony to virtue can come from reformed criminals and repentant sinners. I'm now a retired official, and it's thus reasonable to expect that I'm remorseful and pentitent about the sins I committed while in office. There's some validity to that; and in any case, the perspective acquired during a lifetime in the service of one of the superpowers is necessarily somewhat different from that of a distinguished intellectual or religious leader.

It was suggested that it would be appropriate to comment on "the world situation." I can do that very briefly. It's awful. I don't think any explanations on that one word summary are necessary for this group. What I might ask, however, is that we try to keep this bad situation in perspective. That's what an anniversary like this naturally moves one to do. I'd like to go back another five years for personal reasons, to 1952, when the State Department assigned me to study the Russian language and Russian history, in preparation for serving in our Embassy in Moscow.

Consider then, the state of mind of the US public and US officials in 1952. We were terrified of the Soviet Union. Most of us were convinced that only our nuclear weapons were blocking a Soviet takeover of all of Western Europe. We had a substantial stockpile of nuclear weapons. It was a small stockpile by present standards, and the weapons themselves were still relatively small. But we were ready to use them. And in fact, over the next five years, bringing us to 1957 when the first Pugwash Conference was held, we made a decision to deploy a very large number of these "small" nuclear weapons in Europe, manifesting clearly our readiness to use them. Within a few years there were some 7,000 of them in Europe, and most of these 7,000 are still there today. It is clear that there did not exist at that time any real comprehension in the public mind or even in the minds of officials in the US or in Europe of the character of a war using even a fraction of these 7,000 weapons. There was no comprehension of the immediate effects or of the long-range consequences of such a "limited" war. That sort of limited nuclear war was then considered possible; it was even considered "winnable."

Now obviously, bad as things are today, there are important ways in which they are better. One cannot imagine today a decision like that being taken without any serious public debate. It is not my place here to analyze the changes which have taken place in these past 25 to 30 years in the Soviet Union, but I would be surprised if our Soviet friends disagreed with my view that important changes for the better have taken place there as well, even though—as in the West—things are not quite perfect.

And what of the rest of the world? Thirty years ago and for much of the intervening period, other countries were silent or ineffective observers of the misbehavior of the superpowers. Today, no one who heard the marvelous Philippic which Inga Thorsson delivered to us could describe the role of the neutral and non-aligned countries as silent or passive. There are even some allies of one of the superpowers who speak up from time to time in a critical manner, though in less public channels than those used by the Third World.

What conclusion can one draw from this sort of analysis? I suggest that things really are awful, but that we must—as other speakers here have urged—keep our eyes focused on the future. Modern physics has taught us that everything in the universe is waves, so we should not be surprised if history also has a wave-like movement, not a Euclidean straight line. Philosophers are simply wrong in imagining historical events as forming a straight line, either upward or downward or flat. At this moment, we are in the trough of a wave; but we should not in our depression lose sight of where we are sailing and take our hands off the rudder, any more than we should when exhilarated by finding ourselves on some momentary crest.

It was also suggested to me that I might have some "concrete proposals" to put forward. I'm afraid I don't, perhaps because unlike Ambassador Yakovlev I wasn't able to stay up all night preparing these remarks. But I do have a posture or attitude to recommend. We must not let these bad times lead us to lower our sights and make us accept targets which in better times we would reject. Don't for example, accept arms control as anything but a way station on the road to true nuclear disarmament. Don't be reconciled to deterrence as anything but a condition—a factual state of affairs—which enables us to buy the time needed to work out how to eliminate—totally—the plague that nuclear weapons represent. If we can get rid of the last germ of smallpox, and can truly eradicate that plague, then we can also get rid of the last atom of fissionable material, if that is the only way to deal with the problem of nuclear weapons. This will take a long time—even our children can hardly expect to live in a world free of nuclear weapons; but surely their children should have that possibility. There is no good reason to abandon that hope and that effort.

And to come back to more immediate issues, let us not settle for a START agreement which would be less comprehensive and less effective than the SALT II which an aroused public opinion has now compelled the US Administration to "ratify" *de facto* if not *de jure*.

I offer one very political comment, which will certainly get me the prize for the Pollyanna or the Dr. Pangloss at this meeting. Don't give up—at least not totally—on the current Administration, bad as it is. Its performance has reminded me of Mark Twain's famous comment about his father. He said that when he, Mark, was 17, he thought his father was unbelievably stupid. When he turned 21, he found it quite incredible how much his father had learned in those four years. Like Mark Twain, I am astonished at how much the present Administration has learned about the real world in the past two years. And we must keep in mind the fact that each positive position in the arms control field that is endorsed by the Administration will thereby be made easier to carry through and consolidate in later years. Each of us should do what he can to elicit from the US Government as many useful positions and attitudes as possible over the next two years.

My final comment is to urge that we all reject the pernicious notion that there is a basic antagonism grounded in geopolitics or culture or who knows what, between the US and the Soviet Union. This is the idea that an adversary relationship between the two superpowers is somehow a permanent feature of the international landscape. It is, of course, right to concentrate on the US-Soviet relationship. It is of central importance. And one must acknowledge that it has proved very resistant to efforts to alter it for the better. But it is not unchangeable. It can and must be changed. This is, I think, just as important a task for Pugwash as is the task of devising and advocating technical solutions to the problems of disarmament.

Chairman:

I hope you are all impressed with the wisdom of your chairman in getting Jim Leonard to come here without telling him in advance he had to make a speech, because then he might not have come.

Ambassador James Leonard was for a number of years in the 1960s a senior official of the United States Arms Control and Disarmament Agency and the US representative to the Geneva Disarmament Committee. Later, he was the American representative at the First Special Session on Disarmament, and I shall never forget his official statement on the night the 1973 Final Document was adopted by consensus. He said that we have witnessed a miracle here "and no small miracle at that." Now that he has left government service he is President of the US Committee on National Security—which has an entirely different view of the national security of the US from that of the National Security Council under the current administration.

There's nothing like a reformed sinner, and all people who represent their governments in the field of disarmament, despite having to act on instructions, tend to become committed to the need for disarmament, so that, after they leave their government's service and rejoin the human race, they do marvellous work for disarmament. Jim is doing just that.

- 70 -

PART II

Issues of Disarmament

14. DECLARATION

ON THE 25TH ANNIVERSARY OF PUGWASH

The Declaration which had been provisionally approved by the Canadian Pugwash group was considered by all the participants and guests and a number of suggestions were made for improving the language. These dealt mainly with the dangers of the arms race, deterrence, and pledges of no-first-use of nuclear weapons.

Several amendments to the text were adopted and the Declaration by the Canadian Pugwash Group was approved.

The Chairman announced that the Declaration would be sent to the 32nd Pugwash Conference (25th Anniversary) to be held in Warsaw at the end of August for consideration there.

The text of the Declaration is set out in Chapter 19: "The Declaration and the Linus Pauling Statement", beginning on page 157.

15. THE WORLD DISARMAMENT CAMPAIGN:

MOBILIZING PUBLIC OPINION

Establishment of the World Disarmament Campaign

at UNSSOD II

Chairman:

Mrs. Thorsson has given us a penetrating assessment of the world disarmament situation and of UNSSOD II. One strange aspect of UNSSOD II was that almost all the delegations of the smaller countries regarded the results as a failure and a great disappointment. In contrast, the Western powers, on the whole, said the session wasn't that bad but that we just have to try harder. That was a very interesting change of positions. I suppose that from some points of view it could be said that the Western powers achieved what they wanted there. They didn't want the Session to do anything and it didn't do anything. There were even some who charged that the Soviet Union didn't want the Session to do anything. However, since the Soviet Union came with an important unilateral declaration of no-first-use of nuclear weapons and several other concrete proposals, it is difficult to make that charge stick. UNSSOD II was a disappointment, but not a disaster.

There was, for example, one positive result of the Special Session that has not received nearly the amount of attention that it deserves. That positive result was an important development—it was the official launching of the World Disarmament Campaign and the consensus agreement outlining the guidelines for the campaign. Ambassador Garcia Robles originated the idea of the World Disarmament Campaign and was responsible for shepherding it through the General Assembly to a successful conclusion. Perhaps he can give us some information about it.

Alfonso Garcia Robles:

The World Disarmament Campaign was the only substantive and substantial point on the agenda of the Second
Special Session on which there was agreement. The only
other result was a minor one dealing with fellowships
in disarmament, raising the number from 20 to 25. The
Special Session requested the Secretary-General, who will
be responsible for guiding and coordinating the campaign,
to submit a more detailed report to the General Assembly
this autumn setting out the specifics of the program
for the campaign. But for all practical purposes, the
Campaign has been officially initiated at the opening
of this Special Session of the General Assembly by the
President of the Assembly. There have been a few
pledges of financial support for the Campaign, half a dozen
pledges from governments and also from non-governmental
organizations and from individuals. In the text approved
by the Special Session, the objectives of the campaign,
the contents of its program and the main modalities are
clearly specified.

I hope that during the next session of the General
Assembly, the delegations who insisted on another more
detailed report will come forward with pledges. The
Campaign will then be established on a permanent or
indefinite basis. It is quite separate and independent from
the world disarmament decade. The Campaign will continue for as long as it is necessary to campaign for
disarmament.

Lucy Webster:

I could add a few remarks to give a sense of what is
intended by the Campaign as it stands now. There have
been two documents presented by the Secretary-General
which some countries have argued were not sufficiently
detailed, but they do in fact lay out a number of concrete
proposals. Examples include the production of films,
literature and other educational materials in all the

official United Nations languages for dissemination through United Nations Information Centers in different parts of the world; working with and through members of parliaments, working with professional and other non-governmental organizations; working with educational and research institutes; providing speakers and assisting in the programs of national graoups and improving contacts with and coverage by the media. One of the big controversies in the Working Group that dealt with the Campaign, was whether there would be an international program or whether it would simply be a country by country program. The international program was agreed to by all states; East, West, North and South. This helped to allay some fears in the West about the difficulties of reaching the public in all parts of the world.

Of course the real campaign will have to be what non-governmental groups such as Pugwash do themselves. The United Nations support can at most constitute both a keystone to hold many different initiatives together, and a catalyst to facilitate their effectiveness. But its success will depend upon the degree of public involvement.

Inga Thorsson:

I should like to quote two sentences from one paragraph of the concluding document. "The General Assembly hopes that the World Disarmament Campaign which was solemnly launched at the opening meeting will further contribute to the mobilization of public opinion to the cause of disarmament and the strengthening of international peace and security. In this regard the Campaign should provide an opportunity for discussion and debate in all countries on all points of view relating to disarmament issues, objectives and conditions."

The Center has a Special Political Officer devoted to relations with NGOs. But we were among several delegations at the Special Session which pressed the point that the Secretariat resources must be strengthened. As with so many other points on the agenda of the Special Session, it was not possible to reach any decision during the five weeks on that particular matter. But it will be dealt with at the next regular session of the General Asssembly, and I hope we will have many delegations that then will press for constructive proposals to be carried through by a majority vote if necessary. Strengthening of the role of the Secretariat will be a major item here, and I am certain that this will include strengthening the resources for improving relationships with NGOs and movements like the Pugwash Movement.

Chairman:

Before calling on Ambassador Garcia Robles, I should mention that the First Special Session was addressed by 20 international NGOs and 5 research institutes; at this one there were 53 NGOs and 22 institutes. The role played by people outside the UN was a great deal more active, and maybe in the long run more significant, than the role played by delegations at this Session. One of the hopeful things is that if the World Disarmament Campaign develops as the authors and some of the supporters would like to see it develop, this may be one of the most important decisions taken by the UN in the field of disarmament. More and more people are coming to conclude that no government really wants disarmament except the governments of the small countries. Certainly the nuclear powers and some of the larger industrialized countries behave as though they are paying only lip service to the idea of disarmament because they are doing everything to prevent its happening rather than to make it happen. On the other hand the people of all countries have shown a strong desire for disarmament. The Campaign will help to inform people, and to coordinate their work in all parts of the world.

Alfonso Garcia Robles:

All that has been said by Mrs. Thorssen and by you, Mr. Chairman, I agree with thoroughly. So I will just say a few words to supplement that, to illustrate some of the points. The words "mobilize public opinion on behalf of disarmament," were used in the 1978 Final Document. Some of our colleagues from other countries evidently did not have many constructive things to do so they tried to find some mysterious meaning in the word "mobilize." They wanted to use another word. But we were opposed, as a matter of principle, because we said that what had been approved by consensus in 1978 should be kept. Unless there was some new information not known in 1978, we insisted that we should keep the wording used then.

As has been pointed out, the Special Session had two documents on the World Disarmament Campaign: the report of the experts presented to the 1980 Session (A/36/458), and the other one was the report of the Secretary-General (AS 12/27) outlining very concise, concrete indications of what could be done with the World Disarmament Campaign. The experts rightly said that the World Disarmament Campaign was going to mobilize public opinion on behalf of disarmament. For that purpose, it would need to inform, to educate, and to promote support for disarmament. Those were the three objectives mentioned. And within this context, one could identify whatever concrete measures one wished to achieve those purposes. The Secretariat has given some examples of what can be done. At the same time it has rightly pointed out that what can be done will depend on the resources available. It said, if we were to have $300,000 we could do this; if we had $3 million we could do that, or with $6 million that, and so on and so forth. If we just think of the many millions of dollars that are spent by those non-governmental organizations which promote the opposite ends, I think we will all realize that we could profitably spend as much money as we could get for these stated purposes of the World Disarmament Campaign.

As to how that will be done, it was clearly impossible to discuss in detail during the five week session. Nonetheless, it is already clear from the Report of the Experts which was approved by the 1980 session of the Assembly that the Campaign will be guided and coordinated by the Secretary-General. It is also the general view that the Secretary-General will have an Advisory Council for guiding and conducting the World Disarmament Campaign. It is my personal view, and I have said this in the official meetings that it would be most desirable for the NGOs to be represented on the Advisory Council.

The United Nations and Pugwash

Bernard Feld:

It is not clear to me what sort of follow up a group such as Pugwash should be undertaking in connection with the World Disarmament Campaign. Since the First Special Session there has been very little contact between Pugwash and the United Nations disarmament program. Then when the Special Session took place we were asked to come to New York and I presented a ten minute description of what the Pugwash program is.

How can we avoid repetition of the situation where there is no contact between the two programs which obviously have the same goals until the next Special Session when one of us is asked again to come and deliver a ten minute speech about the Pugwash program?

Lucy Webster:

In answer to Professor Feld's question, I would like to say that I hope that Pugwash, which has great expertise in this field, will not wait to be called on by the Secretary-General. I assume that the Pugwash Movement is so keen on promoting its objectives that it will take advantage of every opportunity to convey its ideas to the Secretary-General and the Centre for Disarmament and will be urging them, as well as Governments, to take the right actions in promoting disarmament. This applies, of course, to all NGOs. If they have good ideas they should be pressing them on all concerned without waiting to be asked.

Chairman:

I agree completely with Lucy Webster. The United Nations isn't going to ask Pugwash to do a thing; it doesn't happen that way. One of the things I have been working for a long time in Pugwash is to have Pugwash tell the

United Nations and the member states what they should be doing. Pugwash is supposed to be loaded with experts and good ideas. We come out with excellent reports from our expert symposiums. They should be, but are not, sent to the UN with a request to circulate them. The statement of the Council at our annual meeting is supposed to be sent to our governments. I phoned two or three leaders of the US government in this field, and I asked if they had received the statement of the Banff Conference. They said no, no one has sent it to them. So I asked Senator Charles Percy, the Chairman of the Senate Foreign Relations Committee, to have the text inserted in the Congressional Record. Although he didn't agree with all of it, he considered it an interesting statement and he had it inserted in the Congressional Record. Pugwash engages in great activity in its meetings; then it often just falls asleep, or it is too busy, or it doesn't have the money to publicize its conclusions. The World Disarmament Campaign gives us an opportunity to get our stuff out to all the members of the United Nations and the NGOs. Perhaps the Centre for Disarmament will take care of some of the expense and the machinery of doing this. I hope that as a result of the World Disarmament Campaign, and as a result of what will be decided on in Warsaw, that the Pugwash Movement will take the required initiatives. It is unrealistic to expect any governmental authority to consult the Pugwash Conference and ask for our help. If we want to help, we must take the initiative, as Einstein and Szilard did with President Roosevelt as regards making the atom bomb. We should move in now to get rid of the nuclear weapons. Nobody asked the Palme Commission to help. They moved in; and that's what we should be doing.

Public Frustration With Inaction by Governments

Georg Ignatieff:

The information from the people who were at UNSSOD II is very useful, but not having been there myself, I am still confused. In the *Disarmament Times* we had the headline: "Disarmament Program Buried, World Campaign Reborn." The thing which struck an outsider was that world public opinion did not seem to need to be mobilized. Rather, world public opinion was mobilized, but the governments required mobilization. They decided to take the usual method of confining the disarmament problem to the three current sets of negotiations—as our Canadian Secretary of State reported.

Far from using the resources of the Canadian Government to help the world campaign, our Government is going to put its money into the old problem of verifying international multilateral agreements. This poses a tremendous challenge to Pugwash. As I understood Ambassador Garcia Robles, the Comprehensive Program for Disarmament (CPD) on which he is working will be completed to be sent to the 1983 regular session.

Now, long before that, several citizen groups in Canada will have voted on the CPD to demonstrate public opinion even before the CPD is voted on by the intergovernmental committee. This shows how the public, in its impatience with the inaction of governments, is taking action on what they believe to be the desirable objectives—whether this is in support of a freeze or a moratorium, or by voting in support of the Comprehensive Program of Disarmament. Thus, the question which comes to my mind concerns the increased impatience of the public. The public is demanding quick action, and drastic action, and even unilateral action in place of slow, diplomatic multilateral and bilateral action. This is where the public turns to nongovernmental organizations like Pugwash for guidance. Also, not expecting to get very much help from their own

- 81 -

governments, they look for leadership from Mexico and Sweden which have provided it over the years.

We have listened to the Secretary of State who expressed faithfully the views of the Canadian Government, the usual attitude of the Western alliance—that they will place their reliance on the time-honored diplomatic approach which has been found to be so inadequate. It results in the conclusions reflected in the statement of the Canadian Pugwash Group that the situation is becoming increasingly dangerous. Thus the public is increasingly looking to NGO groups—and to the Pugwash Movement because of its high scientific reputation. World public opinion is looking for direction and asking: do they support the freeze and a moratorium, do they support a 50 percent cut, do they support a minimum deterrent, do they support a ban on chemical weapons? It is that kind of advice and guidance I think they are looking for.

Mr. K. Subramanyam:

I am not an expert on UN procedure although I was a member of the Indian delegation during this Special Session. Still, going through the session, it was quite obvious from the first few days and the speeches made by the different government leaders who spoke that there was going to be a lot of difficulty in getting any document agreed upon. The first two weeks were used just listening to the standard speeches delivered by the various government leaders. In the third week, the people following the work could already see that there was not going to be an agreed document. So we started making certain soundings, asking whether it would be possible to have a very short document to spell out the major demands and the steps required—since we were not going to have a CPD. However we were consistently met by the response that we shouldn't do this at that time since the working groups were working very hard and we should wait until they came out with their reports. This continued until almost four days before the session was due to be concluded, and it was quite obvious that the working groups were not going to come out with anything and that the whole conference would come out with no result.

We should ask whether the non-governmental organizations and research institutes should not address themselves to preparing governmental delegations in advance for meaningful work, especially if they bring in all the inputs in time. At the meeting of the United Nations Institute for Disarmament Research (UNIDIR) in Geneva in November, I suggested that the proposals of NGOs, research institutes and others should be sent to UNIDIR for compilation, and then sent to the various national delegations by March or April to influence the thinking of the delegations and to focus on certain problems. There was opposition to this from many sources and the main support came from SIPRI and the Yugoslavs. Nonetheless it is important to think of working procedures that would link the work of the General Assembly with the mobilization of public opinion by the NGOs.

To be effective the pressure of public opinion must be felt by the governments. We must go beyond creating the response of Mr. Caspar Weinberger which allows him to brush aside public concern. As Randall Forsberg has said, "we will remember in November." Our action must create effective political pressure that will be noticed.

Today public opinion is fragmented. The NGOs share a common objective, but differ on details. I think the time has come when a major move should be made—perhaps by Pugwash—to unify them into a single world-wide movement. That movement should receive the necessary intellectual inputs. For example, it needs to be made clear why the freeze should come before cuts in armaments. This is especially important when we consider that there are many nations in the United Nations which do not have direct experience of these global strategic problems.

Therefore one can not take the view that public opinion has already been aroused and mobilized. It has to be further aroused and mobilized, so that the impact of it will be felt by the governments concerned especially in the industrialized world. It is there that the NGOs have a major role to play which will be especially effective if they can combine together as an international movement.

Frank Sommers:

I share the frustrations that UNSSOD II brought into our lives. When we ask what use is the whipping up of public fervor, then the answer is that the nations wouldn't be meeting in Geneva now, if it weren't for that. The fact is that the United Nations itself is impotent. If people lose hope in the United Nations, that weakens the one international structure which exists for resolving conflicts and tensions.

Consequently, I think there is a great danger in disappointed expectations. I had no sense that the urgency which those of us outside the UN building felt was in any way shared by those who were inside. But a sense of unresponsiveness is what gives rise to frustration, whether it is seen in the superpowers or in the United Nations.

So, UNSSOD II was a profound disappointment. Many of us in Canada tried to give focus to our speeches and work throughout the country, using UNSSOD II as the rallying cry for people to put their energies into letting our government know what should happen at UNSSOD II. A lot of energy went into that and was wasted. The Canadian Parliament had a special committee which spent all of February listening to 50 or more groups from across the country. They came to Ottawa and gave testimony on their concerns and on what the position of the Canadian Government should be at UNSSOD II. A long detailed report was prepared. There was also a short Minority Report signed by six members of Parliament representing all three parties. While the minority report caught people's imagination, and there were many expressions of support for it, most people do not know what the Government's position was in the main report of the Committee. Likewise most people are not aware of what the Canadian Government did at UNSSOD II. I don't know how it is in other countries, but if it's the same kind of apparent lack

of responsiveness by the Governments, then this will increase frustration and disappointment, and will lead to two
results. A number of people will conclude that this is a
game which only politicians can play and will lose interest;
other people will become more angry, and perhaps even
more violent if they feel strongly enough.

Paul Cappon:

My professional work is medical and also social. Unlike
most of you here, I am directly involved in a grass roots
movement, as Chairman of the Nova Scotia Coalition
Against Nuclear War, which is the umbrella disarmament
group for the whole of the Maritimes. We have, already,
37 constituent organizations. What happened outside the
United Nations during June is perhaps more important than
what happened inside. What we are doing in our rallies and
in our pressure work in the various public disarmament
groups across the world may be more significant than what
went on in the United Nations.

It is beginning to be clear now that we are looking
for guidance, not from governments, but from the non-
governmental organizations and the public.

We have heard about the need for greater mobilization
of public opinion. In our own particular small area of the
world, support for our coalition already represents the
majority of the population in the Halifax area. A majority
of the citizens of Halifax and of Nova Scotia support a
nuclear-free zone in Canada. The scale of our mobilization
is not being matched by the effect we are having at the
political level. Perhaps it never will be. We need the
visible help of important non-governmental organizations
such as Pugwash. More guidance will have to be provided
by the Pugwash Movement and by similar non-governmental
movements in concert with grass roots organizations, which
you here are saying should play an increasing role.

What I propose specifically for the Pugwash Movement
—and this echoes two proposals already made:

- One, that there should be a unifying role played by Pugwash in a single world-wide movement for disarmament as Mr. Subrahmanyam proposed.

- Two, I think that the Pugwash Movement should apply direct political pressure itself. This sort of pressure should be asserted in a permanent and continuous way—not just intermittently. I would suggest that perhaps a permanent committee should be formed within Pugwash to do this on a continuous basis.

Role of the Public:

Elections, Education and Secrecy of Negotiations

Ian Carr:

This is almost a one sentence question following on the last two speakers. When we mobilize all this public opinion—and there are many people whom I assume are working very hard to do this—how do we harness it? Is there another way of getting this punch into the system to affect events, other than by the electoral process, or are we mobilizing public opinion to go out and participate in the electoral process? I don't know the answer to the question. It's a question which I think sociologists in a group like this might try to answer.

Chairman:

I'd like to make two comments on that. Number one is that you certainly have to work through the electoral process. You have to be politically active and work at the constituency level. It's much more important to work on your own MP than to work on the Cabinet Ministers or Prime Minister who just sends your letters off to some bureaucrat to answer. But if your own MP gets the impression that a lot of people are really interested and concerned, he will pay attention. Number two is that we have to find some way of getting through to the media. Dr. Cappon said that physicians need Pugwash. I would say the reverse has been true. Pugwash needed the physicians to wake up the people of the world. Pugwash certainly hasn't done it. I am one of those who has believed for a long time that there is a role for Pugwash in helping to inform and educate and mobilize the public as well as governments. But so far I haven't been very successful in promoting that point of view. So I say we have to do what we are doing, but we have to work much harder, and we need to get the media involved, and we need to be involved in the electoral process.

Ian Carr:

But is there anything more? You see the question I am asking. There are hundreds of people across the country doing these things. But I am asking, what else can we do.

Sergei Kapitza:

I would simply add that there is the educational process. Educating people in schools and in the broad public is a long term process that affects the public's underlying point of view.

Lucy Webster:

Having a real effect is partly a question of having a clear and simple unified message: for example, freeze, plus cuts, plus CPD. But you need a depth of understanding also. People need to really understand the issues if they are going to be effective in speaking to their MPs. That's where education comes in. There is a whole story to learn.

Chairman:

The UN report on the World Disarmament Campaign talks about working through schools, universities, governments, parliaments, NGOs, media, professional groups, church groups, etc. The United Nations has moved a long way since the expert report initiated by Ambassador Garcia Robles in 1979 in getting the whole thing laid out on what can be done. Those of you who are interested can easily write to the United Nations and get a copy of that expert report and of the two additional reports submitted by the Disarmament Centre to the Special Session.

Herbert Scoville:

I strongly support the view that getting into the electoral process is probably the most important technique. In the United States, what happens in the elections this November will have a very important effect on where we go—although I am not optimistic that we will turn the present Administration around no matter what happens.

I would like to mention one other thing. I think the biggest issue that we all have to face today is that there are attempts being made, I believe, to silence the anti-nuclear sentiment, and to bury it in the secret, private negotiations in Geneva, both on the European nuclear weapons and on the START talks. Such negotiations do, of necessity, have to be private to a certain extent. But I think we all have a very important task in keeping our negotiators and our leaders honest by making sure that they are seriously negotiating, and not just going through this process as a means of quieting the anti-nuclear movement.

This is not an easy task because the Administration will claim that they can't talk publicly because that would jeopardize the negotiations and results. Nonetheless, I think we have to find some technique of having enough information made available. On the other side—the non-governmental groups opposing SALT II were very effective in getting information during the SALT II negotiations, and they essentially sabotaged the treaty by the way they used this information.

Our aim would not be to sabotage the talks. Rather, it is to keep them negotiating honestly and to demand concrete results now—not five or ten years from now. By then we will have gone through another whole stage of developing and making dangerous destabilizing weapons.

Inga Thorsson:

I just wanted to emphasize the point which Mr. Scoville was making. As Swedish Chief Negotiator for Disarmament, I have never experienced such a frustrating situation of not having any access whatsoever to the bilateral talks. Always before, in the SALT talks or whatever talks were going on bilaterally, we have always been able to sit down, in confidentiality, and to have some information, to know what is happening and what progress is being made. Now we are absolutely closed out. The strictest secrecy is imposed in the START negotiations; we don't even see the negotiators. This is a very dangerous situation in my view. Exactly as Pete Scoville said, they can just sit there behind closed doors to appease the anti-nuclear movement and not do anything in reality. We have to develop a technique by which we can at least have some basic information as to what is going on so we can keep the public awake, in the future as it is now.

16. THE NUCLEAR FREEZE

John Polanyi took the Chair

Scope of the Freeze

Chairman:

When it was suggested that we discuss the freeze at this session, I was told that the freeze is the hottest thing around. Certainly it is in the news. The proposal itself must be about four months old—at least in its most recent incarnation. On this continent it takes concrete form as the Kennedy-Hatfield proposal of March 1982.

It is a freeze in the testing, the production and the deployment of nuclear weapons. Those are the operations to be frozen. There are also three things to be operated on: warheads, missiles, and delivery systems. The freeze proposal has a second part, that the USSR and the United States should, after the freeze, pursue major mutual and verifiable reductions in warheads, missiles and delivery systems by an annual percentage.

The freeze is a relatively catchy, simple and dramatic proposal which can be explained in a way that can be readily absorbed. A second virtue is that verification becomes easier when you have an agreement that is broad enough.

As for faults; one that is stated is that it doesn't go far enough. This is usually stated by people who privately think the freeze goes too far. This is my personal analysis of that fault. The second fault is that it removes the incentive to disarm. This is somewhat baffling. If an incentive to disarm comes from a continuation of the arms race, then one or the other of the superpowers should have been disarmed some time ago. In other words I don't see the logic of that argument. Instead people have thought that the incentive to disarm came from two sides: disarming and seeing the other disarm.

Ten years ago in 1972 there was a vote taken on a freeze proposal and there was strong support for trying to negotiate a freeze. There have been proposals for freezes made by the Soviet Union. For example, in 1978 the Soviet Union proposed a freeze in the United Nations. It was initially a quantitative freeze, but became a qualitative freeze also in a statement by Mr. Gromyko to the General Assembly about a year ago. So both kinds of freeze have been covered in proposals by the Soviet Union, and these are important declarations of intent. Whether both sides will continue to support these ideas when it comes time for both to do so simultaneously, I don't know, but we can hope so and can try to facilitate that.

The scope of the freeze proposal also deserves further comment. The scope is broad and subsumes various other proposals. For example, you can't have a freeze on testing without having a Comprehensive Test Ban Treaty. That is part of the freeze as I understand it. You can't have a freeze on production without having a ban on the further production of fissionable materials.

We should discuss whether a ban on the testing, deployment and production includes a ban on the replacement of bombers, ICBMs and submarines which carry ICBMs. But here there is an area for discussion. And what about defensive systems? The Soviet proposal I mentioned specified both offensive and defensive systems. One can also ask what about conventional weapons—especially since there are various sophisticated delivery systems which could be used with these even after they were banned for use with nuclear weapons. So those questions relate to the scope of the freeze.

I should say just a little more about verification. Many people assume that the prime method of verification which is used for all existing arms control agreements—national technical means—would not be sufficient for an agreement of this magnitude. People therefore speak of "black boxes"—a favorite Pugwash topic—and of on-site inspection. In both those areas there has been a very marked softening of the misgivings of the Soviet Union. Thus it is no longer idealistic or wishful thinking to talk about black boxes or on-site inspection. The question now is, when and how?

Duration and immediacy are also important issues relating to the freeze. Immediacy is important so that the nations of the world don't start to think of actions to undermine an agreement and have time to institute those actions before such an agreement exists. So one would like the agreement to be reached soon. In order to achieve an agreement quickly, maybe one should aim at something of two years duration. Such an agreement of two years could, perhaps after one year, be translated into something of five years. There are all sorts of possible views about duration.

The final point I will mention for discussion is the reduction-phase sequel to the freeze. The Kennedy-Hatfield wording talks about reductions by certain percentages every year. If you read that now in conjunction with the statement of both superpowers that they will abide by SALT II ceilings, the fixed percentages begin to sound like a proposal that was made in 1979 in the US Senate, that a phased reduction should be a reduction from SALT ceilings, keeping the framework of SALT during the reductions.

This is all intended to stir things up for our discussion.

Joseph Rotblat:

One other point which I think we should discuss is the opposition to the freeze and the official reasons for which some governments do not accept it. It is important that we understand these reasons so we will be able to answer these questions.

Rod Byers:

I think we all understand the opposition of the Reagan Administration, and also the opposition by NATO, and more specifically by certain European countries. Within that context, I think the opposition stems in part from the question of the scope of the Kennedy-Hatfield proposal in as much as it encompasses the entire spectrum of nuclear weapons and calls for a global freeze of all nuclear systems.

In that context, some consideration has to be given to the American position regarding the Intermediate Range Nuclear Forces (INF) negotiations. I have some sympathy with the NATO position and the arguments by the Reagan Administration that, if they agree to the Kennedy-Hatfield proposal, that is going to complicate the negotiations in Geneva on INF. This concerns the question of the SS-20s and the intermediate nuclear forces balance in Europe. At the Banff Pugwash Conference last year, the Soviet scientists indicated that they would not consider reducing the number of SS-20s unless it was clear that NATO was going to go ahead with its program for Pershing II and cruise missiles. That aspect of the Kennedy-Hatfield proposal has to be addressed.

Is there any point in trying to split the freeze proposal between strategic nuclear weapons, and issues concerning other types including battlefield and intermediate range nuclear weapons? If you separate the European situation from the bilateral superpower situation, the arguments that are being presented by the Reagan Administration against a freeze become much weaker, since there is no imbalance of strategic nuclear systems. I agree, however, that once you get into separating the INF negotiations from an overall freeze, it is much harder to explain to the public. There would be legitimate concern that the freeze would only be a partial freeze.

In my view the Reagan Administration is not likely to agree to a freeze of any type.

The differences in the American and Soviet perceptions of the nuclear balance are fully set out in the 1981 US publication, *Soviet Military Power,* and the corresponding Soviet publication in 1982, *Whence the Threat to Peace.* Each superpower is accusing the other of trying to achieve nuclear superiority, and of following policies based upon a

nuclear war fighting capacity. Recent American statements about "prevailing" in a "protracted" nuclear war
make their positions clear. Each superpower is also
accusing the other of producing destabilizing trends by
developing increasingly accurate counterforce nuclear systems. One can turn to any number of figures to show that
the nuclear balance can be measured in many different
ways in either European or global terms.

Until agreement is reached between the two superpowers on how they perceive the strategic environment,
you are not going to get anywhere on the freeze or
anything else. This is one of the reasons that I tend to be
very pessimistic, at least for the next two years. Consequently, one of the things I would like to see Pugwash do is
to try to bridge the conceptual gap between the two
superpowers in terms of how they perceive the strategic
environment. If we can do that, and convince the public
and the people involved in decisions, that they are talking
past each other, then I think we will have moved the
debate a step further where they can really start talking
about freeze proposals without having this automatically
rejected by the Reagan Administration.

Chairman:

Just on a point of information on the first half of what
you said, the freeze proposal which I had mentioned was
debated in the US Senate a dozen or so years ago, was in
fact the John Sherman Cooper proposal, and it actually was
a proposal for a freeze on strategic weapons of all sorts. It
did make the division which you were saying perhaps might
be made between strategic and European nuclear forces.
This was discussed in April 1970 and approved in the Senate
by 73 votes to 6.

Herbert Scoville:

In 1964 the Johnson Administration made a proposal
at the Eighteen Nation Disarmament Committee for a
freeze of all strategic delivery vehicles and that included

research, development, production, testing and deployment. That was an official proposal put forward in Geneva, but it was not picked up at that time by the Soviet Union.

I think the main objection made to the freeze is the one that Rod Byers has raised, that the West cannot afford to have a freeze now because we are in a position of strategic inferiority. That is the central argument being used.

There is not much disagreement on the facts concerning the force levels of both sides. Everyone is working from the same data base. But everyone is selectively choosing this or that part of the data to prove what he is trying to prove, a preconceived notion that we are ahead or we are behind or that we are seeking superiority. Both sides play this game. As was mentioned, there are booklets published by each side claiming that the other side is superior.

I personally think that there is a perfectly good balance. I think deterrence against nuclear attack is the only excuse for nuclear weapons when they exist. And I think we do have a strategic mutual deterrent balance now where there is really no conceivable threat of a first strike. That is the essence of the situation. If you recognize that fact, then it is clear that both sides can afford a freeze now.

I think all of us must make clear that if we stop today, there is no immediate threat to the security of either side. We don't have to buy more weapons to make sure there is a deterrent against an attack.

Paul Cappon:

I think there are two overriding reasons for adopting a freeze proposal. One is that the so-called modernization of nuclear weapons which would actually be a qualitative change in nuclear weapons is the greatest danger to security. It would be an even greater danger than an increase in numbers of weapons. In that sense the technologists are leading the strategists who are leading the politicians and the scientists down paths that will soon be irreversible.

It is not the numbers themselves that matter. As was noted earlier, we could reduce the number of weapons by 50 percent, 70 percent or 80 percent; and it wouldn't make any real difference. So freezing at the present level is not so much a question of numbers as everyone here knows, but the important point is that we would freeze qualitative changes and thus stop the extremely dangerous upgrading and improvement of nuclear weapons. That is the over-riding advantage of the freeze.

A second advantage is of even greater importance. The freeze is not only a question of numbers and qualitative change; it is above all a question of attitude. One has to be able to reestablish the kind of climate of confidence that was present, to some extent, ten years ago. What is needed is a climate reasonably free of suspicion, a climate in which it is possible for a step to be taken, whether bilaterally or unilaterally, with a reasonable degree of confidence that the other side will follow. The freeze is one way of establishing an adequate level of confidence that the measures we initiate are serious and that we are bargaining in good faith to achieve eventual reductions.

Finally, I wish to comment on the idea that there should be a bridging of the gap and some sort of persuasive mechanism to alter the way in which the politicians and diplomats perceive the strategic environment. That approach seems to assume that they don't create the strategic environment, which of course they do. I would argue that our role should be more pressure than persuasion, and that, if we have to bridge a gap right now, the gap that we have to bridge is between the freeze proposal position and the uninformed public.

Joseph Rotblat:

While I agree that it is basically a political issue and that the arms race is madness—and we have said so in Pugwash many times—I also think that as scientists we should go a bit further than making a general political statement. We have to be able to support, on scientific grounds, any proposal put forward, and to answer any criticism made about the freeze.

We must first be clear that the whole question of parity and superiority is nonsense. It doesn't matter whether there is parity and superiority because, as long as both of the major military nations can absorb a first strike and still be able to destroy the attacker, then the actual number of weapons can be reduced by a very large amount without changing the reality that there would still be a devastating second strike capacity. That is the basis of deterrence.

There are several common fallacies which we in Pugwash have pointed out at our conferences. One is the fallacy of thinking that nuclear war can be limited whereas, in fact, any nuclear attack or exchange is very likely to escalate into a full-scale nuclear war. The second fallacy is to talk about any problems of parity. A few hundred megatons is all that is required for mutual deterrence, and the present arsenals consist of tens of thousands of megatons.

Sergei Kapitza:

I agree with the point just made about the fallacy of thinking there can be superiority when you have the enormous overkill capacity which exists. Nonetheless, the idea of parity provides a clear way to present the message to the public—that numbers don't matter because there is essential parity and balance in strategic weapons. I think this is an important message to get across that may contribute to the freeze negotiations.

Also, I think the freeze issue should be connected to the concept of no-first-use of nuclear weapons. We need to find a way to establish this connection. This would lead to discontinuing the arms race in an operational sense, and you would end the idea of using these arms, and then you can go to the further stage of reducing them.

I think it's important to get these basic goals fixed. If the freeze were actually about to happen we could then, at that time, go into some of the details.

Jim George:

Although we may be frustrated by 30 years of negotiations which have not led very far, it is important to not give up on negotiations at this stage. In about a year and a half from now we will be in a situation where we won't be able to verify nuclear arms reductions, and therefore we won't be able to reach negotiated disarmament agreements. I am speaking of the time when NATO will have deployed cruise missiles and when satellite surveillance will no longer be enough to give us a satisfactory degree of mutual verification.

If we are really facing an 18 month deadline on negotiating disarmament, I think we ought to be leaning hard on governments through public opinion in every way we can to insist that those negotiations in the time remaining be very serious and very urgent and very specific. Maybe the freeze, if it is not to detract from the negotiating process, could be reduced a bit in scope and focus on the real problem of the next generation of nuclear weapons and delivery vehicles—including especially cruise missiles which are the most invisible of all from the satellites. I am in favor of a freeze, but I don't want to reduce the impetus to negotiate seriously in the time we have left to stop the development and deployment of cruise missiles.

Chairman:

Perhaps I'm not close enough to this topic to comment, but I imagined that the freeze would involve some rather difficult negotiation. It would have to be a mutual and verifiable agreement. It could conceivable be a result of reciprocal unilateral action, but I thought it was contemplated primarily as something that does involve negotiation and rather skillful but urgent negotiation.

K. Subrahmanyan:

I think it is necessary to address ourselves to the point that the objections to the freeze proposal will have to be addressed. But in doing that, I think our statement will have to be more than political. The question can't be dealt with simply by saying that so long as there is capability to absorb a first strike and retaliate, that there is parity, and that it is thus possible to reduce weapons by freezing and then negotiating cuts. One has to address oneself to the argument about nuclear superiority. One even has to go into the question of absorbing a first strike and whether a first strike would make sense. I did raise this subject in the conference of the International Institute of Strategic Studies with General Rowny. I asked whether he thought that it would make sense for the Soviets to use all their land-based heavy missiles to take out all the US land-based missiles, and what would be the consequence for the Soviet Union of exploding 6,000 or 7,000 warheads over the continental United States; and, secondly, whether it was feasible to do it, that is to say, whether such a first strike can at all be carried out. His answer was, "I agree with you, it cannot be. But, I have negotiated with the Soviets for a thousand hours; and I believe that they believe that they can do it."

It is not only a question of getting down to the details; it is a question of perception about the other side, or of the perception that each side wants to convey to its own population to support its political stand. Therefore one has to tell the public that what is being discussed is not always the real feasibilities and the real capabilities, but that people are attributing certain capabilities to others according to the perceptions which they wish the public to believe. This is the point which Pugwash, as a scientific community, is in a position to tackle. We should first question whether carrying out a first strike is at all feasible; or whether this is something that is totally impracticable.

Sergei Kapitza:

I want to interject a point, regarding the concern over first strike capacities. This concern is not valid any more since the no-first-use commitment has been made.

William Epstein:

The overall situation is one of rough parity. The real deterrent in Europe isn't in intermediate-range European weapons; the real deterrent is in the strategic weapons, where there is clearly substantial parity. And it is this strategic balance that in the final analysis will deter any nuclear attack or threat in Europe. It is claimed that the biggest problem as regards a freeze is in the INF situation in Europe where the Soviet Union has some 300 SS-20s with some 900 warheads, while the West has no comparable intermediate range missiles. I think that has been greatly exaggerated. There are four US Poseidon submarines allocated to Europe with 160 strategic nuclear weapons on each one, providing 640 warheads; there are four British Polaris submarines, with three warheads on each of 48 missiles, making a total of 144; there are also five French submarines each with 16 missiles, which have one big warhead each, making a total of 80 warheads. Thus there is a total of 864 nuclear missile warheads on Western submarines in Europe. In addition, there are the forward based airplanes which carry nuclear weapons and I believe the West has a definite advantage there.

Hence, if there were a total freeze on the introduction of all nuclear weapons the West would not be at a significant disadvantage even as regards the European situation.

Unless we can achieve a nuclear freeze, then the INF and START talks become largely meaningless. Without a freeze we shall be faced with the whole range of horrible new weapons: MX missiles, B1 bombers, cruise missiles, Trident II missiles, and of course, new Soviet missiles too. The US Administration says "let us negotiate the zero option in the INF talks and reduction in START and then

- 101 -

we can freeze." That is not a freeze, but an anti-freeze, and it won't work. It permits the technological qualitative arms race to go on unhindered.

In any case, neither the freeze, nor the INF talks, nor START are going to succeed in the next two years under the present US Administration. If we are fortunate, the situation will change after November 1984. In the meantime, we can be preparing the ground both for a freeze and for subsequent reductions. And our efforts might even have some restraining influence on the current US Administration.

Paul Doty:

I was an initial signer of the petition for the Kennedy-Hatfield Resolution when there weren't many people in the arms control community who would do that. I worked on its formulation and had some successes and some failures. In the end everyone likes to support his own freeze, and the problem is to get a common definition that is sufficiently precise to have meaning and not so overly precise as to be burdensome and turn off the public. Remembering past freeze proposals and their negative reception should tell us that success is not going to be automatic. Thus, those of us who have background in these matters have an obligation to move it beyond its present ill-defined stage to what could be doable in a rational world and then try to push for this.

If one reads the Kennedy-Hatfield proposal, and believes in the words, "verifiable" and "bilateral," and if you want to do something quickly, I think it is almost a certainty that you are driven to a scale of action that is not very far beyond what SALT II was. Even that modest affirmation is by no means useless, because of the recent indications that its terms will be followed even in the absence of ratification, so long as neither side violates its terms. I think the next testing period of our relationship in the arms race, will come in three or three and a half years when the SALT II Treaty dates will run out. Thus the most fundamental kind of freeze that I would like to see would

- 102 -

be an indefinite continuation of SALT II requirements until something takes their place. If we don't take advantage of the possibility of having that kind of stability, we will be ignoring the chance to have a relatively easy victory for this particular part of the freeze.

Then one has to ask what one can do quickly beyond SALT II. As John Polanyi reminded us, the ban on nuclear testing is much discussed but lying dormant. Stopping production has been less discussed, but is more difficult to agree on and verify; so this brings us back to deployment which has been the focus for action and effort, and which could follow SALT II and provide a basis on which to build other action.

It seems to me that in trying to give greater definition to the freeze concept, one has to give priority first to deployment, and then to testing and then to production. I don't think it is possible for existing governments to reach bilateral and verifiable freezes on all three of those things within this year, and probably not next year. So one has to scale down one's expectations to a phased approach, and try to correlate the contents of each phase to what could be doable in one year or two years or even three. I think a freeze on production, considering the extent to which the production is unknown on one side by the other, will take years to reach a stage where it will be verifiable. I wish myself that production were not a part of the freeze.

Finally, I think it would be useful to examine quite different alternatives to a freeze. I could imagine that after a year and a half, if the START negotiations have stagnated, and the public recognizes that it may be appropriate to think of a different kind of freeze, that could be immediate and would cover a stated number of areas where deployments were about to begin. Such a freeze on deployment could, on a temporary basis, be based upon national means of verification with each side able to withdraw on one month's notice if its intelligence indicated the agreement was not being obeyed.

There is a greater measure of flexibility in the freeze concept than is often conveyed. To insist that there must be a freeze that includes everything, would be deceiving the public whose interest is now so thoroughly aroused.

Derek Paul:

I first want to come back to the way the freeze would affect the INF negotiations. I wonder whether it isn't possible to stop the testing and production of the cruise missile. Once the cruise cat is out of the bag, it is going to be a very difficult one to control. So it is particularly important to stop the production of cruise missiles as quickly as possible. I accept the statement that stopping production has not yet been considered in sufficient detail, and this is something to which we have to address ourselves.

Bernard Feld:

One can certainly verify a freeze on the production of fissile materials for weapons use, but on the other hand, production of components for delivery vehicles of various types would be more difficult to verify. So the main problem with the freeze as I see it concerns what it is that you want to freeze. The most satisfactory kind would be a complete across-the-board freeze on everything relating to nuclear weapons and their stockpiling. But then one would get into a myriad of problems—if one is going to proceed by negotiation. A bilateral, negotiated freeze would be a process that would take the lifetimes of most of us here.

There is one aspect of the situation which is extremely important, and here I would refer to the remarks of Sergei Kapitza. We are particularly concerned with the possibility of a nuclear war breaking out and with the first use of nuclear weapons under various possible circumstances. This could be due to accident, preemption, or for other reasons. Hence, I wish to emphasize the importance of introducing the no-first-use concept into the freeze discussion at a very early stage. The delegitimation of nuclear weapons seems to be crucial if we hope to avoid their being used, and if we are eventually going to stop producing them and eliminate them.

I would like to tie the no-first-use concept together with a freeze on systems which it is generally agreed are predominantly of interest for preemptive uses, which are in fact first-strike systems. Now, I think it is possible to define some aspects of this problem in a reasonably straightforward way, that is, to discuss freezing preemptive or offensive nuclear systems, such as the highly accurate ones with very large warheads since these are the ones we have to worry about most. If that kind of freeze were tied to the concept of no-first-use, it would be a major step forward.

David Cavers:

Paul Doty anticipated a kind of concern which had not come much to the fore in the first enthusiasm for the freeze. In supporting the freeze, we should recognize that this is a process that does not occur instantaneously and that in the design of a freeze appropriate recognition must be given to the problems of the verification of the matters to be frozen.

The emphasis placed on stopping deployment is one that certainly can be viewed with enthusiasm as a starter. There is a problem in advancing an idea of this sort that we combine a concept of genuine advance over the current situation, together with the recognition of the fact that we are dealing with a very complex operation and are therefore not expecting a miracle to occur with the waving of a wand or the signing of a document.

Sergei Kapitza:

I would simply like to use this occasion to elucidate the statement that was made this spring by Premier Brezhnev. He referred to the importance of coming to terms on a freeze, on the strategic arms of the USSR and the USA, as soon as any talks begin, and limiting their modernization to the utmost. He further proposed that, as long as the talks lasted, each side should take no action capable of leading to any upset of the strategic situation. Such a freeze, important from the point of checking the nuclear arms build up, would also substantially facilitate headway towards a radical reduction of strategic arms. I think this clarifies some of the points we were just discussing as regards the Soviet position.

William Epstein:

I, too, was an original endorser of the Kennedy-Hatfield resolution on the freeze, but I have a somewhat different approach from Paul Doty.

Verification, as we all know, has been used more times in the past as an obstacle to agreement than as a means of facilitating agreement. If you want 100 percent foolproof verification, this is almost impossible. If you merely want satisfactory verification, so that there is a high confidence in detection and a low risk that anyone will be able to get away with anything, that is easy to get. In the past my experience has been that any time an agreement is wanted, questions of verification disappear. The prime example is the Biological Weapons Convention, which is completely unverifiable, so they let it go at that, without any verification procedures. SALT I and II rely on national technical means and this was considered adequate and satisfactory.

With respect to this particular proposal, a freeze on testing, production, and deployment of nuclear weaons, it is very interesting that William Colby, the former head of the CIA, who is not likely to be easily bamboozled, told the Senate Foreign Relations Committee that such a freeze can be satisfactorily verified.

If you ban all testing, production and deployment, meaning that you close down the plants, then it is fairly simple to verify a ban on production because these are large plants, and there is no way you can produce much fissionable material without its being detected, especially through the cooling towers. With satellite surveillance, you can even see the traffic going in and out of these plants just as the satellite cameras saw, or thought they saw, the preparations for an underground nuclear weapon test in South Africa, even though the structures they were building were pretty small. If you take into account the other national means of verification such as telecommunications monitoring, other electronic sensors and good old-fashioned spying, then I would think that verification does not pose any insuperable problems.

It is much more difficult to verify limitations or reductions of selected weapons or to verify the number of remaining weapons or vehicles. But if *all* new production is stopped, then it really is relatively simple. Take the traffic in and out of plants; if they are all closed down, either they are going to have to be reopened or new ones will have to be built. It is possible to verify an under-ground test ban better than anything else, down to one or two kilotons. And yet the United States keeps saying that they cannot agree to that because of verification problems. Governments are using the remote possibility that someone will get away with an isolated little explosion or two as a means for blocking the whole agreement. The real reason is that they don't want the agreement. It is a question of political will. If you want a freeze, you can get it. The question of verification is not simple, but the problems involved are not so difficult that they cannot be overcome. But there is one proviso—we must stop the production of cruise missiles before they are produced in substantial numbers; they are so small that I do not think they are verifiable.

I personally do not think that the Reagan Administration will agree to any kind of freeze—neither a total freeze nor a partial freeze limited to deployment of strategic weapons or even of the most destabilizing strategic weapons. They insist on first building up their excessive nuclear arsenal. So I think it is better for us to support and promote a total nuclear freeze so that a new Administration would be in a position to agree to one quickly.

I agree that it will take years to negotiate any treaty on a freeze, even on a partial freeze. I am becoming convinced that Jerome Wiesner, Linus Pauling, Garcia Robles, Inga Thorsson and others are on the right track when they urge that a freeze can be achieved, at least as a start, by mutual national actions.

Theodore Hesburgh:

We have been discussing what I consider the most important moral question that has ever faced human beings because this is the first time in the history of humanity on earth that we can literally reverse creation and destroy ourselves. If there is a declaration from this group, I'd like to join it.

Looking to what you are going to be talking about this afternoon and the future scope of Pugwash, I think you have a great reputation to build upon. I think what the public has learned to look for from this organization is sensible enlightenment. Sensible enlightenment is extremely important in view of the enormous public movement which no one can quite explain—it is like spontaneous combustion. This movement is just there, and it is growing, it needs focus, it needs direction, and from time to time it needs some sensible advice.

So I would hope there will be a word of enlightenment in whatever we say. First, we are not faced with all the discontinuities concerning superiority and parity. In fact, there is overkill parity. And since this does exist, we can move ahead on a program. We are facing destabilizing developments and we have to avoid these and move ahead or future negotiations will be eliminated because of the nonverifiability of the weapon systems now being created.

I hope that whatever we say will cover the final as well as the beginning elements. The beginning is the freeze, and the final element is the complete elimination of the nuclear threat to humanity. I think it has to be said that that which we are ultimately seeking, that which alone can allow us to sleep easy at night, is to get this threat totally eliminated.

There are four steps that are often mentioned here. First there is the freeze, which is something that might be done rather quickly. It must be meaningful and not just pie in the sky; also it must be verifiable; and also it must be bilateral since the central focus here is the USSR and the USA.

The second step needed is a no-first-use pledge. Thirdly, reduction has to be constantly mentioned with the freeze. And lastly we must move toward elimination, and at that point, action would be more than bilateral.

I think we have all this enthusiasm in the world today, facing this problem, wanting desperately to do something, but it needs direction, and it needs rather simple direction. People have to know that this is a time we can move. The Soviets aren't going to be insecure, and we aren't going to be insecure if we move now. I would hope somehow, through rather informal discussions, we have got to get to the President of the United States and Premier of the Soviet Union, and I think we have to say to both of them, that together they must sit down and each say to the other how far each could go, and how far they could go together. They could both arrive with a shopping list. We could write the shopping list right now for both of them for a meaningful, bilateral, and verifiable freeze. Secondly, they would need to agree that the sort of calamity that could happen by accident requires that there be some safety mechanisms in place, plus a pledge of no-first-use. Thirdly, let's immediately start talking about reduction, let us not either of us send the two biggest hawks in our country to have those talks, but let's get some people to act who really are going to be serious about getting reductions.

And lastly, let's keep before us this fundamental aim, that we are going for the elimination of the nuclear threat. Unless we do that, all the conversation is useless because a few years from now there won't be anybody left to talk.

Negotiations or Unilateral Initiatives

Alfonso Garcia Robles:

We conceive of the freeze as a means of obtaining concrete results soon. We do not wish to embark on interminable negotiations which will make a freeze possible in 20 years. It is in that perspective that Mexico and Sweden have put forward a complete draft resolution on the freeze at the United Nations Special Session on Disarmament. Since no consensus was attainable on any substantive issue we asked that our draft resolution be sent to the 37th Regular Session of the General Assembly this autumn.

We do not view the freeze as an end in itself, but as a means, as an instrument. We think that at present there are two very urgent objectives to achieve. The first objective is "to stop any further increase in the awesome arsenals of the two major nuclear weapon States which already have ample retaliatory power and a frightening overkill capacity." The second objective is spelled out in the following way: "Believing also that it is equally urgent to activate negotiations for the substantial reduction and qualitataive limitation of existing nuclear arms." We believe that the freeze is the most effective first step that can be taken for the achievement of those two objectives, "since it would provide a favorable environment for the conduct of the reduction negotiations, while at the same time preventing the continued increase and qualitatiave improvement of existing nuclear weaponry during the period while the negotiations would take place."

We think that, with good will on both sides, this is a feasible proposition. The present United States Administration seems to have found that the freeze is a good procedure. In the Jackson-Warner proposal there is nothing against the freeze. The only reservation there is that, and I quote, "Whereas the current nuclear balance is destabilizing and could increase the likelihood of war." That is in the preambular part. Then, in the operative part, it doesn't speak of increasing the weapons of each side; it just says,

"A long term, mutual and verifiable nuclear forces freeze at equal and sharply reduced levels of force." Consequently, what the present United States Adminstration has found wrong with the freeze is not the procedure or the concept; it is just that it contends that at present there is a terrible imbalance that must first be rectified.

Is there an imbalance in nuclear forces? I think that in the eyes of Pugwash, and in the eyes of all those who have objectively examined the present situation, that is not correct. At the Banff Pugwash Conference it was said that at present there is a rough parity in the nuclear forces of the two superpowers. That was specifically concluded in one of the working groups where Ambassador Ignatieff and I were the co-conveners. More recently the Palme Commission, the Independent Commission on Disarmament and Security, came to conclusions along exactly the same lines as those of Pugwash in Banff. In addition, there was a lengthy article in the New York Times by Leslie Gelb who was in charge of an arms control section in the State Department for several years under Secretary of State Cyrus Vance. In his recent article he examines the strength of recent armaments, field by field and sphere by sphere: submarines, navy, aviation, bombers, missiles, everything—including also the information and communications capabilities. His conclusion is exactly the same as that of Pugwash in Banff, and of the Palme Commission. So we must accept that there is rough parity, and consequently, there could not be more propitious circumstances for a freeze. Thus, that is one important element regarding the freeze: to maintain that it is feasible at this time.

A second element which deserves our attention concerns verification. Rightly, it has been said that in disarmament, verification is indispensable, but not all types of verification are equally practicable. Thus it is important to note that it is easier to verify a complete freeze than to verify some limitation of the type contemplated in SALT II. I believe Mr. Scoville has written several pieces on this point. That is why, in the draft resolution submitted by Mexico and Sweden we have a paragraph where it is said that the freeze, would be subject to all relevant measures and procedures of verification which have already been agreed by the parties in the cases of the SALT I and SALT II treaties, as well as those accepted in principle by them during the preparatory trilateral negotiations on the Comprehensive Test Ban held at Geneva.

As you know, for almost four years, beginning in 1977, the United States, the USSR and the United Kingdom carried on those trilateral negotiations concerning the CTB, and in those negotiations, they accepted informally, in principle, several measures of verification, even including some on-site inspection. Thus the SALT and the CTB provisions show what could be, in our opinion, seen as adequate and duly verifiable measures.

I would add that, in my opinion, the freeze should include the production of nuclear weapons. The Final Document of UNSSOD I, in its main paragraph concerning nuclear disarmament, which is paragraph 50, speaks of

cessation of the production of nuclear weapons and their means of delivery and of the production of fissionable material for weapons purposes.

Finally, to conclude as I began, in our opinion, a freeze, if there is good will, is feasible, the conditions could not be more propitious, and no prior negotiation is required. It will be enough, as we suggested in our draft resolution, to act

either through simultaneous unilateral declarations, or through a joint declaration.

Ian Carr:

I would like to ask Ambassador Garcia Robles why he spoke of having a freeze on the production of both weapons and delivery systems. This takes us into an area which is very difficult. Therefore I wonder if you would have anything to amplify your statement as to why it would be feasible and not too problematic to freeze the production of delivery systems; I am especially wondering what you would include in delivery systems.

Alfonso Garcia Robles:

I am not an expert who could describe to you precisely what should be included there. If it was possible in connection with SALT I to establish certain prohibitions which I think are more complicated to verify than a total freeze, I don't see why the delivery systems should not be included.

Ian Carr:

The reason I asked the question relates to the present concern over cruise missiles.

Peter Scoville:

Air launched cruise missiles were included in SALT II, with verification.

Alfonso Garcia Robles:

I think we must make proposals on the basis that there will be good faith and good will. The first thing both sides will need to do is provide complete data on everything that the freeze covers, as they did in the case of SALT II. There they agreed on how many missiles, how many bombers, etc., how many missiles are MIRVed, how many are not. This data would be provided at the starting point to state precisely what the freeze covers.

Lucy Webster:

I have a question for Ambassador Garcia Robles. You said one doesn't require any prior negotiation; the resolution simply refers to joint declarations, or unilateral declarations. I don't quite see that a declaration is an act, or how you can get away from negotiation, and how one can implement a freeze instantaneously. Obviously you can make an instantaneous declaration, but how do you actually produce an instantaneous freeze?

Alfonso Garcia Robles:

Well, actually it will not be instantaneous. It will take one week, or two weeks. What do you have to do? You have to proclaim, either through simultaneous unilateral declarations, or joint declarations an immediate nuclear arms freeze of which the structure and the scope would be the following. It would embrace a comprehensive test ban for nuclear weapons and their delivery vehicles, the complete cessation of the manufacture of nuclear weapons and their delivery vehicles, and no further deployment of nuclear weapons or their delivery vehicles, the complete cessation of the production of fissionable material for weapons purposes. Each side could provide data in 48 hours.

Linus Pauling:

I must say that, as one of the two surviving signers of the Russell-Einstein Statement that led to setting up Pugwash, I am especially pleased to be able to participate in the 25th Anniversary Celebration of the First Pugwash meeting. I am more concerned than ever about the possible destruction of the world as we know it through a great nuclear war. In thinking about these very serious questions, I have formulated a statement that expresses my own opinion as to the actions that the people of the world, and especially of the two great nuclear powers, should be urging upon their governments.

If you will allow me, I shall read this; it's only about 100 words.

> The danger of world destruction in a nuclear war is now greater than ever before because of the escalating arms race between the United States and the Soviet Union. To halt this race, I urge that a treaty be made by these two superpowers to freeze the testing, production and deployment of all nuclear weapons and their delivery vehicles, with the freeze to be followed by major reductions. Because making a treaty is a slow process, I urge that these powers immediately take unilateral actions to institute this freeze, to be supplemented then by international agreements as soon as they can be formulated and ratified.

I am glad to present this statement which I have prepared to this 25th Anniversary Pugwash Meeting and I look forward to having the benefit of your discussion of it and your advice.

Ian Carr:

I think that this group might well get into detailed discussions about what to freeze and how to freeze it and how long this would take. However I am not certain that a sensible statement with such details can be produced in one day. What I would very much like to see is a brief and a clear and concise statement on the freeze put out by this very well-informed group. I would like to bring your attention back to the statement of Linus Pauling which I think puts the matter simply and clearly.

I find it difficult as a doctor to understand words like those I have heard around this table, such as "capability to absorb a first strike". I think that when we use language like that, we distort our perception of reality. We distort our perception of 100 million dead human beings. I don't like that kind of language, but I can understand the language of world destruction in a nuclear war. So I hope that this meeting will agree on a resolution very much like the one prepared by Dr. Pauling. I think that we should understand that the Pugwash Movement can have a slight but very definite effect on the public. We can give the broad public movement additional credibility.

I would ask that we look at one word in Dr. Pauling's resolution. That is the word, "unilateral." I myself am very happy with unilateral actions, but I have always been conscious that unilateralism is not something that goes down well with the public.

I would like to see a brief sentence added, at the beginning of this resolution, saying that there is presently approximate parity in nuclear weapons between the super-powers. I would also like to see in the resolution clear support for no-first-use. However, while I think this important, I think it is probably impolitic at this stage.

I think the freeze is simple, straight forward, and I think we should go for it; and in words like Dr. Pauling's. And lastly, I for one am not willing to scale down my expectations.

John Polanyi:

I welcome the fact that there is a certain polarization of views here. We are faced with a fairly massive public movement. We are delighted and we want to capitalize on it. The question is whether realism demands that the freeze be interpreted as being something that goes very little beyond SALT II, or whether realism demands that it go considerably further, because only then do you get the benefits of really achieving something visible, and at the same time making verification simpler.

Focusing the Freeze Debate

Frank Sommers:

Just a few points. I keep getting confused and I think many of the public keep getting confused. I quote from the Department of Defense Posture Statement for 1982, page 42:

> While the era of US superiority is long past, parity, not US inferiority, has replaced it. The United States and the Soviet Union are roughly equal in strategic nuclear power.

I don't think the United States public has been told that sufficiently by the political leadership and the impression of those of us at the sidelines, like some of us in Canada, is that there are political games being played with these weapons, both internal politics and external. It is Kennedy's plank now to push the freeze, and I think that by definition, that makes it unacceptable to Reagan.

Last year in Banff, the Russians were indignant when it was suggested to them that their SS-20s were destabilizing the situation. They said they were acting in self-defense: modernizing their SS-4s and SS-5s in response to the NATO forward-based systems. So the escalation continues. There does appear to the general public to be a striving by both sides for unilateral advantage and superiority. Soviet leaders such as Marshal Ustinov have said repeatedly that the USSR will not accept inferiority. Nor will the Americans.

Thus the whole world is held hostage to the military planners. This is a political issue, and if Pugwash has any influence, it has to have some impact on the political outcome.

The freeze is simple to understand whatever form it takes. It makes sense to people when they hear repeatedly that each side has enough weapons to destroy our world 20 times over. This is madness.

Isn't it time that we as scientists and physicians, people with a reputation for thinking, say that the madness has to stop? We should add our voice to whatever proposals are coming up, and we should not get embroiled in the minutiae. We must not lose sight of the urgency of the situation. Nor should we forget that many people have serious difficulties appreciating the technical refinements of the claims and counter-claims made by people who are jostling each other for political and not merely military gain.

The value of Pugwash lies in the fact that we are an international organization of scientists from many countries and we are not interested in the political or military gain of either side. With increasingly destabilizing weapon systems on the way, the urgent task for us is to come out with a clear voice endorsing the freeze concept.

George Ignatieff:

I hope that this group will not go back on the Banff position that a nuclear freeze is an essential part of any strategy at this point. The difficulty is one of how much emphasis to put on the technical problem of the cruise missile with regard to verification. This question has not been fully addressed although it was mentioned in SALT II. As Leslie Gelb has written:

> There is no sure way to verify a cruise missile's range, no way to tell whether it carries a conventional or a nuclear warhead, and, apart from being a potential nightmare for the strategic balance, cruise missiles affect prospects for achieving reductions in other nuclear weapons.

This does present a problem. Ambassador Garcia Robles suggests that to have a comprehensive approach to a freeze you must achieve it quickly or face the fact that cruise missiles, after they are produced in quantity, have to be specifically excluded from the freeze because of the verification problem. Another problem is the political one. I don't think we can realistically propose a nuclear freeze in the present state of rhetoric which suggests that before we can freeze or come to any kind of conclusion on any negotiations, we must overcome the alleged superiority of others. I think the mere mention that there is strategic parity is one of the calming elements. I think we as scientists and political scienitists can contribute to the process of de-escalating belligerent rhetoric.

Rod Byers:

I'm not suggesting that we should step back from the position taken at Banff supporting a nuclear freeze. But we should, perhaps, use this discussion to lay the ground-work for what we do at the Warsaw meeting next month. I'm not sure it is in our interest to come out with another brief statement on the freeze in the hope of affecting public opinion. The most recent New York Times poll on this question indicates very clearly that two thirds of the American public support a bilateral freeze. What I do think we should do is to have Pugwash come out with a statement at Warsaw indicating why a freeze is viable. Our aim should be to go beyond a short simplistic state-ment of support, but to prepare something to be presented to governments as well as the public.

Chairman:

To discuss why a freeze is viable we need to define exactly what one has in mind by freeze, and that is what we have been beginning to discuss. Certainly, to influence our governments, we must go beyond the point at which the public debate seems to rest at the moment which has a tremendous enthusiasm for the freeze, but which does not provide a very explicit statement.

17. THE FUTURE OF DISARMAMENT

AND A NUCLEAR FREEZE

George Ignatieff took the Chair

Chairman:

We now have an associated topic to cover: the relationship or link between a nuclear freeze and other measures related to disarmament.

The issue of disarmament is no longer regarded as just a technical issue, but as an issue affecting people's survival, economic livelihood, economic development, and also as being intimately related to security. Therefore it is not just the things which States refrain from doing of a military nature which matter, but also the things which are done in cooperation on a global scale.

Robert Reford:

I wish to return to the point which Father Hesburg made that we are on the eve of destabilizing developments in the arms race. In a sense, we have always been on the eve of destabilizing developments in the arms race, and some weapon systems have turned out to be less destabilizing than others and many have been less destabilizing than was anticipated at the time. It may in fact be true that all new weapons are destabilizing when they are first introduced, then when they are matched by the other side they become less so.

Nonetheless, I think we ought to look at some of the technological questions. The problem of verification of cruise missiles is one new development. We also have the question of anti-satellite weapons and Prof. Kosta Tsipis*

---

* Reproduced in Appendix 2 at page 167.

has presented us with a very excellent paper on that. There is the likely development of laser weapons. Nobody has talked about anti-submarine warfare today, but we keep on hearing that one of these days there may be breakthroughs in anti-submarine warfare which may spoil the present invulnerability of missiles carried on submarines.

Mr. Trudeau in his address to the General Assembly repeated his proposal for a technological freeze; he also mentioned the need to negotiate a treaty to ban weapons for use in outer space. I emphasize the words "for use" which he had in his text, because if you talk about weapons in outer space, that does not include weapons based on the ground or in the air for use in outer space. So those words, "for use," are very important. This is an area to which we should be devoting our attention—the link between the nuclear freeze on the deployment, testing and development of nuclear weapons, and some kind of freeze on technological developments. This is the sort of thing to which scientists in Pugwash ought to be turning their attention. We should be pressing governments to follow the pattern of the Anti-Ballistic Missile Treaty to see whether we cannot produce other treaties or agreements to ban that sort of technological development.

Banning the Use of All Weapons in Outer Space

John Polanyi:

Bob Reford raised the point about the need to follow the freeze with a ban on weapons for use in outer space, which can be conventional and not nuclear, but extremely destabilizing. I don't know by how much we are able to delay such a ban. If it follows the nuclear freeze, it may be delayed too long. This is part comment and part question. We have a brief memorandum that was sent to us by Kosta Tsipsis at MIT which is a sort of catalogue of coming weapons for use in space. The most immediate one of those is the anti-satellite weapon which is enormously disruptive, and I should think totally senseless because it's going to be equally disruptive for both of the major contending powers.

So the first question is, how long do we have? I would like to address this to people who are in touch with these things. How long do we really have in which to try to implement the suggestion made by Mr. Trudeau at the Second Special Session. I think there is a very real possibility of making the superpowers come to the realization that it is very much in their interest to close the gate on that sort of development. I understand that the USSR has also proposed to ban all weapons from outer space.

The second question is a technical question on how hard would it be to verify a ban if it were introduced six months from now, and how hard would it be to verify if it were introduced 18 months from now. The question that I have concerns how fast things are moving with regard to anti-satellite weaponry. I heard it rumored, as we probably all have, that the Soviet Union has an early-generation anti-satellite device which is shot up from the earth and which explodes in space and could be used as an anti-satellite weapon. The United States is developing a miniature homing vehicle which is described in that sheet of Kosta Tsipsis and which has not been tested. But when will it be? Presumably, this will happen some time in the coming year. And, once tested, how easy is it to reassure people that it's not being manufactured? The deployment is a rather trifling operation of strapping it under the wing of an airplane. I think this is a subject that Pugwash might come to grips with.

Dr. Ogawa:

With regard to nuclear disarmament, I would urge my American colleagues to consider the importance of international backing more seriously. I am afraid that the notion of a freeze is not at all well-known in Japan and is also not so familiar in Europe. I have heard much about the mass movement in Germany, Holland, and so on, but the point of the anti-nuclear movement there seems to be rather different.

In a meeting such as this we should exchange more information with each other. And I wish to say that in Japan, even among scientists, the notion of a freeze has not been discussed as deeply as here. I think that the notion of a freeze is too vague, and thus, that such a proposal could take too long a time to realize. On the other hand, a proposal such as the CTB, or for a pledge of no-first-use of nuclear weapons, are very concrete so that it is possible to realize such proposals in a very limited time. However, if you take too much time in defining our own proposal, it will require more time for politicians to accept such an idea.

Although I do not oppose the freeze concept, I don't really understand why American scientists are so eager to discuss and support it. I cannot help but wonder whether there would not be some easier program which Pugwash should develop and itself support.

Paul Doty:

I would like to add to what John Polanyi said about an anti-satellite treaty. The discussions were broken off nearly three years ago and the various initiatives that have been restarted or put on the table did not include an anti-satellite treaty or the test ban treaty.

There are two quite different technological approaches to anti-satellite weapons. One is to have a weapon which would seek out a target and destroy it. That involves launching facilities, and because of the few possibilities which exist from any launching base to launch and intersect an object in existing orbit, the rate at which such a target could be hit is rather slow—probably a matter of days. Therefore, if this kind of aggression began, the other side would be tempted to consider it an act of war and bomb the launching sites from which the original attack came. So some sort of defensive protection would have to be built into that system, which may make it less possible for it to become a decisive instrument.

The other approach mentioned, to launch it from an airplane, is under development. This involves a problem of accuracy since there are about 5,000 large objects in space right now, and therefore the problem of intercepting a particular one from an airplane is quite a feat, and there is a risk of hitting the wrong target. So that approach will probably require a longer experimental development stage, but once perfected, would certainly be dangerous in that it could wipe out all of the targeted satellites in a short time.

So I certainly support the sense of urgency, but I think it depends more upon political will than upon any technical solution that could be proposed. As regards the space shuttle, it is a space transport vehicle and it can transport anything that weighs less than 65 tons. So it is just like asking whether a truck can be a military vehicle. And of course the answer is that it can. Space shuttles represent a development in space technology which is irreversible and it will come to be a commonplace means for transporting large weights into orbit. I don't think there is much one can do about it since one can hardly ban the shuttle itself any more than one could ban trucks on earth.

John Polanyi:

As I read the documents of the Geneva Committee on Disarmament, this matter of outer-space weapons is on its agenda these days. But I suppose it is not really on the Soviet-American agenda.

Priority for the Nuclear Freeze

Sir Mark Oliphant:

I wonder whether we can not settle this question of the freeze on nuclear weapons first before we begin to discuss details of technology. It seems to me that these questions are all peripheral. If we agree that a freeze is desirable, I think we should have the courage to say so. We shouldn't hedge it round by saying that perhaps the cruise missile will be the fly in the ointment. I'm quite certain that this difficulty of detecting the cruise missile is being made too much of. Whenever the cruise missile is brought out of its hanger or its container to be used, it will be detected by satellites within a very short time; and it will certainly be detected when it is in flight. Although you can't easily detect it by ground-based radar, it is easy to detect it from satellites.

I wish we could make up our minds whether or not we support, without reservation, as a first step, a freeze on the production, testing and deployment of nuclear weapons and on the vehicles to deliver them. After we have done this we can then talk about any snags that may develop, but I am quite sure that none of these are of any magnitude at the present time. They may become so because of technological developments, but let's get the freeze in before those developments take place.

George Ignatieff:

I should mention that we do have the statement of Linus Pauling and we need to consider whether to adopt it as a resolution or not. But I suggest that we keep that to the end so that we can deal with the substance.

Alfonso Garcia Robles:

I think we should concentrate on the question of the freeze and, after that, we can discuss whatever disarmament measures we like. We could discuss outer space and also chemical weapons which are very important.

We have the freeze proposal put forward by Dr. Linus Pauling, and perhaps we could take this as a basis. It is generally acceptable to me but I would suggest two changes.

First, what the people of the world wish—and I think, most governments also—is some concrete result in the near future, urgently, not within 50 years. If we are going to have the freeze by means of a treaty, I am afraid that in 20 years, we would still be discussing its terms. I would instead suggest something along the lines of what Mexico and Sweden put forward in their draft resolution in the recent UN Special Session on Disarmament, that is for the US and the USSR to proclaim the freeze, either through simultaneous unilateral declarations, or through one joint declaration.

The use of the word simultaneous makes it quite clear that there cannot be just one unilateral declaration. This simultaneous approach has been used in the past several times. The United States and the Soviet Union can talk, not for years, but for one or two weeks and agree to issue simultaneous unilateral declarations proclaiming the freeze. That is one possibility.

The other possibility is to have a single joint declaration which would be the result of bilateral consultations. This might take from one to three months. So this point about timing is my first observation. The freeze can be initiated by two simultaneous declarations, or by one joint declaration within a matter of weeks or months.

My second observation is that Dr. Pauling's resolution has the advantage of conciseness—as compared to the Mexican-Swedish resolution. It is shorter, and to the point. My only suggestion would be to add something on fissionable materials for weapons purposes. Earlier I quoted from paragraph 50 of the Final Document of the First Special Session on Disarmament which provided not only for the cessation of the production of all types of nuclear weapons and their means of delivery, but also of the production of fissionable materials for weapons purposes.

Some Western countries, Canada in particular, were in favor of stopping the production of fissionable material, and the Soviet Union has always said that this was all right, but that we primarily need to stop the production of nuclear weapons. Consequently, the compromise was to put them together as in the wording of the Final Document which I have just quoted. So I would also suggest that addition to our document.

Flora Lewis:

Not being a scientist of any kind, I am here as a consumer. I am perplexed about the whole issue of a freeze. It is not self-evident to me that it is a wonderful thing. It is self-evident to me that nuclear war and nuclear weapons are bad things. But I have a lot of questions as to why or whether a freeze is a good way of improving the situation. Scientists might be expected to help us consumers to figure out what we are really talking about, and what it is going to do to us, what the chances are for it, and whether it can work and how.

The whole debate on the nuclear freeze until now—certainly in the public—has been an emotional one. I think the emotional need for limiting, and reducing, and eliminating nuclear weapons is very widely understood. What is not understood, and I myself don't understand, is why this or that way of going about it is preferable, and how it will work. And I also wonder whether you are not cutting off some scientific development that would make the question of stability and the question of security better rather than worse.

I understand the word "freeze" to mean stop, no more nuclear weapon activity. But it isn't self-evident to me that all activity in this field should stop. I come back to the point that Pugwash should perhaps be giving

- 128 -

information rather than merely giving encouragement to a general emotional position.

Joseph Rotblat:

If you are referring to military activity, I would simply say this: no military activity is better than some military activity. But I do agree with your second point—that we should provide more information on this matter.

The Legal Status of Unilateral Declarations

in the United States

David Cavers:

With respect to unilateral declarations for a freeze, I am not entirely sure what the status of those would be in terms of the authority of the President to bind the United States. It would seem to me that such a declaration would be a statement of governmental policy, but would not have the Senate approval which would be required for a treaty. Maybe it would be accepted as an international agreement.

Herbert Scoville:

On this subject as to whether you can have government actions which do not require Senate confirmation, I think you can. After all, we have such decisions all the time on whether to go ahead with this or that weapons system—which is essentially what we are talking about here. The President can make that decision. If the Congress insists on voting money and saying it has to be spent for a specific purpose, then there is a constitutional argument. In general, the President can make a national decision to, say, not go ahead with the MX program. There is nothing that says he has to buy the MX.

Robert Reford:

Do I understand you correctly as saying that if there were two unilateral declarations, one by the United States and one by the Soviet Union, this would present less of a problem than if there were a joint declaration by the two countries?

Herbert Scoville:

I think that's probably right. Furthermore, I wouldn't call them unilateral, either. In fact, I wouldn't even call them declarations. What I would do is to speak of "national action." The President can do certain things or not do certain things as part of national action.

David Cavers:

I think the important point is that such action should be described and taken in such a way as to not be confused with exercising the treaty power.

Disarmament Must Start with a Stop

Bernard Feld:

There is ample evidence from the past 30 years that when negotiations are accompanied by attempts by the negotiating parties to improve their positions during the negotiating process, the negotiations do not get anywhere. By the time any progress is made in the negotiations, the things about which they are negotiating become obsolete.

What we are talking about is mainly a principle. In my view the principle of the freeze says that one has to accept that when one starts negotiating about any specific system of arms—nuclear, conventional or whatever—that the beginning of the negotiations should be accompanied by an agreement not to change the status quo during the negotiating period. That's what a freeze means. To me the principle is extremely important because it is the violation of that principle which is in a very large measure responsible for the failure of any effort for arms control and disarmament for the last 30 years.

Linus Pauling:

In the escalating arms race, two nations are spending more and more money and developing more and more complex and dangerous systems. It is proposed that they stop testing, deploying and producing nuclear weapons and fissionable material. This does not mean that new ideas cannot be heard, but during a freeze they should not be ideas that involve changing the nuclear weapon system. But there could be ideas that help prevent nuclear war. I think it would be good if we had a period of time during which weapon systems did not escalate and when there would be concentration on world problems. In the context of a moratorium, peace could be discussed. I don't believe the freeze would interfere with that kind of progress.

George Ignatieff:

The reason the freeze is needed is that the technological pace of innovation in armaments is always ahead of
negotiations by a long stretch of several years and the
problem has always been to find a way to hold up the
innovation. The fact is that the innovators in the labs
continue to innovate. That is what led to the Canadian
strategy of suffocation, which is one form of a freeze—a
technological freeze.

Sir Mark Oliphant:

We must recognize that disarmament discussion has
virtually no future and no meaning unless we start with a
stop. A freeze is needed for the start of fruitful disarmament talks; it is not the beginning of disarmament.
Once one has that out of the way, then one can start to
reduce the number of weapons. But until one has stopped
this wholesale helter-skelter path to destruction, one is not
going to be able to agree on disarmament. The weapons
which are the subjects of disarmament talks change from
week to week, so until one has a stable starting point as
the basis for talks, there will not be any criterion for
beginning.

Linus Pauling:

I should like to address the subject of the future of
disarmament. I agree with Sir Mark that the future of
disarmament would be much brighter if there were to be a
stop to the escalation first. That is one way to get started
on the future of disarmament. Secondly, it seems to me
that the future of disarmament would look brighter if we
gave up our complete dependence on the formulation and
ratification of international agreements. Consequently, I
would like to hear ideas expressed about the idea of
unilateral actions, some of which have already been taken
by the superpowers. I would like the idea of unilateral

action to be discussed carefully, and perhaps some recognition could be given by Pugwash to the possible value of this approach. It is clear that things just go along too slowly when the process gets in the hands of the negotiators.

William Epstein:

I agree with those who say that you have to stop a car or a ship before you can put it in reverse. I think the proposal for a freeze, whether it is the Kennedy-Hatfield resolution or the Garcia Robles, Inga Thorsson resolution at the United Nations, is much clearer and more specific than either the Reagan proposals for SALT or the Brezhnev proposal for a freeze. Certainly, they are much more clear than the statements which either superpower makes about a Comprehensive Test Ban. It is an old, old technique, and I'm not accusing anybody here, but I have listened to them all so long that the technique becomes very clear—if you want to block progress on something, you insist before you start on so many details that you kill the thing, or you insist on so much verification that you kill the thing. The important point is to get the negotiation going on the subject that you are talking about. I think the Swedish-Mexican proposal is so straightforward and so complete that nobody can have any misconceptions:

1. A comprehensive test-ban of nuclear weapons and their delivery vehicles.

2. The complete cessation of the manufacture of nuclear weapons and their delivery vehicles.

3. A ban on further deployment of nuclear weapons and their delivery vehicles.

4. The complete cessation of the production of fissionable materials for weapons purposes.

Those provisions are so clear and specific, that, if you really want to make progress on the freeze, you have everything you need. If you don't want to discuss the freeze, you can of course raise more and more questions.

I also like the Pauling proposal. It is short and simple, and it is understandable. I'd like him to change two words: "unilateral actions" to "national initiatives." National initiative means substantially the same thing, but may not arouse the same constituency of automatic opposition.

Alfonso Garcia Robles:

I am aware of the fact that the binding nature of unilateral national actions is much less than for a treaty, but I would be happy to have such declarations even if the binding force is less than for a treaty. It is that which we have in mind for our resolution in the United Nations, and that is also what I would suggest for the draft of Dr. Pauling.

Decision on the Linus Pauling Statement

Chairman:

There are a few participants here who were not in favour of Dr. Pauling's resolution because they favored a negotiated freeze. During the coffee break Ambassador Garcia Robles, William Epstein and Linus Pauling attempted to draft a revised statement for possible adoption at this meeting. Several straw votes indicated that the revised draft also could not obtain a consensus but the majority supported the idea of sending the revised statement to the Pugwash Conference at Warsaw for its consideration there but not to release it anywhere else.

Alfonso Garcia Robles:

As I understand our proceedings, we decided that the revised statement initiated by Linus Pauling would be transmitted to Warsaw. May I make the following proposal on which we could take action.

> The 25th Anniversary Commemorative Meeting of Pugwash held in Pugwash N.S. in July 1982, decides to transmit the attached statement initiated by Linus Pauling to the 32nd Conference to be held in Warsaw with the recommendation that it be taken into account in the preparation by the Conference of any text concerning this matter.

Chairman:

The proposal is adopted by consensus. [The text of the statement is set out in Chapter 19: The Declaration and the Linus Pauling Statement.]

18. THE POLITICAL ROLE OF SCIENTISTS

AND THE PUGWASH MOVEMENT

Chairman:

We shall now move on to the last item on our agenda and discuss the role of scientists and of the Pugwash Movement in the political field.

Providing Leadership

Margaret Fulton:

It is the public which must stop the arms race. It won't be the governments that act regardless of any resolution that comes from this meeting. It will be the gradual buildup of masses of people who will get to their politicians. They will put such pressures on governments, the kind of thing that happened on June 12th in New York, that governments will finally act. What the people out there need is precisely this kind of statement which will give them authoritative support. It will legitimize their own efforts. This statement by Dr. Pauling on the freeze is exactly what the people outside of Pugwash are looking for. They are looking to the Pugwash thinkers and scientists to make a statement that will confirm for them that they are on the right track when they march to ban the bomb. Then people will say it isn't just a lot of anti-nuke kooks; you see the thinkers at Pugwash and the professionals are giving us the authority and confidence that we need. Certainly, what the people need is a statement which is short and simple. It is what the media can handle, and it is what is needed to give the grass-roots peace movement around the world the sense of conviction that they need to keep on doing what they are doing, which is to keep on getting to their politicians, and thus to force governments around the world to take seriously a freeze on nuclear arms.

Frank Sommers:

Regarding the future of disarmament, it may be that our future is already behind us. That is a rather chilling thought, but I speak from the perspective of someone who is part of the clean-up crew. I am also very involved in International Physicians for the Prevention of Nuclear War, and the mobilization of doctors across this country and other countries.

It seems to me that the problem we are trying to tackle is basically psychological, and the question in people's minds is whether all the technological wizardry which scientists have developed in the name of protecting our safety is not in fact endangering our safety. So science does not have a very good track record when it comes to this issue. This is the view of the people, especially the young people, who are now concerned about the military uses of science. At the same time I have the impression that many young scientists are devoting their lives to the development of weapons.

But if the problem is psychological, then we should ask ourselves what we can do to enhance people's security. The people in the West should know there is a better choice than to become red or dead, and people in the East should know they will not be overcome by the forces of capitalism.

People want some substantive answers, some national understanding that they can hook into and take to bed at night so they can sleep well. They want to know that a freeze is acceptable because of a precise list of concrete reasons. It may be a very useful contribution for this kind of group to develop a program or a document along that line. Of course the Arms Control Association has done something along that line in terms of analyzing the freeze proposal, and a number of other proposals, setting down the pluses and minuses of each.

However, my concern is that all of this may be no more than a game of intellectualization and rationalization, and, if we are running out of time, then there is not much time to play these games. It seems to me that the popular movements all over the world, such as those inspired by Physicians for Social Responsibility, may make whatever we do here irrelevant.

It seems to me that the negotiation processes that are going on don't have to take years, and that it would be possible to negotiate quickly if there were a will to achieve results. The negotiations are games. That is why they take years. And people are getting fed up with that. That is my experience. That is what I have observed. There is a sense of urgency as well as of frustration. It may be that a group such as Pugwash can reduce the frustration and help people develop a sense of direction. One form our work might take could be as a detailed scientific document as to why a particular arms reduction proposal is useful. If we can do it that way, then let's do it. In that way we can provide support and assistance to the popular movements and, through them, to governments.

How Pugwash Functions

Joseph Rotblat:

I wanted to speak on the Pugwash Movement. We have had a number of suggestions at this meeting on what Pugwash should become and do, starting with the Statement from the Secretary of State for External Affairs. It is quite natural and helpful to have these suggestions. Nonetheless I wish to point out that if we implement an idea for a new approach, we can produce something new, but this transformation also means that something else may be lost.

That something we might lose may be a vital feature of the organization—one that is essential for its effective continuation. Even if we achieve something spectacular in an appeal to the public, this could turn out to be short-lived, because in the process the basic reason for the organization may be lost. We have to be very careful when we think about changes.

This is not a plea for conservatism. Pugwash is certainly not conservative; we are the most elastic body I know, our committees change constantly, we have no constitution, no membership, a minimum of bureaucracy; thus we are ready all the time to accept changes.

I would not like it thought that I am against mass movements or that I depreciate public opinion. Before the era of the present mass anti-nuclear movements, I remember preparing a list of possible new steps for disarmament. I noted that these steps would have to be accepted by governments, if they were to be implemented, but that governments would not act unless forced by public opinion.

Thinking recently about the 25th Anniversary and the meaning of the First Pugwash meeting, gave me an opportunity to look again at what sort of features are very important for us but are in danger of being eroded. I would like to mention three of these which are in fact linked.

Bertrand Russell insisted from the beginning that, apart from Pugwash always having scientists from both East and West, we should also cover the whole spectrum of political opinion. And this did happen at the first Pugwash Conference. The fact that such a gathering was able to agree on a detailed and substantive statement on very sensitive and controversial issues is due to a large extent to the personal stature of the participants. One characteristic which linked all these leaders was that they were great scientists who had made important contributions in their own fields. They were recognied by the scientific community as top people, and the scientific community listened to them and respected them. I believe this is the crux of the matter for Pugwash. We are a movement of scientists. This is the origin and raison d'être of Pugwash. Our title is Conferences on Science and World Affairs. It is this input of scientists on world problems which is unique to us, and this is an essential characteristic of Pugwash which we must keep in mind. I stress this point because there seems to have been some erosion in its importance. For example, we have had fewer and fewer natural scientists coming into Pugwash. During the last 5 years less than 30% of newcomers were physicists, compared with the first Pugwash meeting where 70% of the scientists were physicists. It isn't just the numbers, it is the quality which concerns me even more. We no longer seem to have the very top scientists coming to our meetings. This struck me very painfully during the past year when Brezhnev made his proposal to set up an International Committee of Eminent Scientists to investigate the consequences of a nuclear war and to find the means of averting any such war. This is almost word for word the terms of reference by which we were set up 25 years ago. But now it seems that Brezhnev felt that a new Pugwash, as it were, was needed because the present Pugwash no longer fulfills the function. Fortunately the Pugwash Council has realized this shortcoming and has recently made an effort to bring back top scientists into Pugwash. In Warsaw we are going to have a declaration issued which will update the Russell-Einstein Manifesto. And, incidentally, this will include support for the freeze. This declaration has been sent out to Nobel Prize winners in physics, chemistry and physiology. I think that about two-thirds of the people to whom we sent this have replied, and all but a few have agreed to sign the declaration. So I hope this will be the beginning of a new trend by which we will be able to speak with renewed authority—especially to speak to other members of the scientific community. There are literally hundreds and thousands of scientists involved in military research, and a very small proportion are concerned about these matters. This is our first task—to arouse the scientific community above all. I do not believe it is our task to go out as a movement to become a public forum. What we should do is to make sure the scientists become educated and that they go out and speak to the public.

Once again, I can say we have made a start on this. Recently we have prepared a book, *Scientists on the Arms Race and Disarmament*, which will be published jointly with UNESCO. This book calls on the scientific community to undertake specific action:

- to give their time and thought toward these objectives,
- to elaborate specific steps of arms reduction,
- to give earlier warning of dangerous new developments,
- to collaborate with current medical campaigns that are informing the public of the consequences of nuclear war.

I think this is our main task, and to be successful in this task, we must have the top scientists so that what we say will be accepted by the scientific community.

A second characteristic of Pugwash which I consider essential is our independence and individuality. We come to Pugwash conferences representing nobody but ourselves. And, insofar as our main task is to provide an informal channel of communication between East and West, this channel must remain informal if it is to fulfill its function. In this way we were able to keep going even when official East-West channels were ruptured as happened during the

Vietnam War and the Afghanistan conflict. In this connection I want to express my regret that the American Pugwash Committee attempted to stop us from holding the 1982 Pugwash Conference in Warsaw because of martial law. By going to Warsaw we do not condone the military regime in Poland any more than we condone any regime in any country where we hold our meetings. We are not a political body, and I think it is important to keep Pugwash as apolitical and as independent as it has always been.

The third point which I believe we must remember concerns the atmosphere which we maintain in all our meetings. When Cyrus Eaton greeted us in his formal opening address at the first session he said,

> When you go back to your respective countries,
> I hope you will think of the other fellow as a
> friend, as a man with whom you can work and
> admire.

I believe that Cyrus Eaton was not disappointed in this respect. Although we have always argued with each other on important issues, we have also developed personal relationships and a strong bond of friendship and trust. It is essential to maintain this characteristic of Pugwash. And if there were ever any conflict between growing in size and maintaining the quality of closeness and trust, then priority should be given to upholding the strong bond of friendship and closeness and trust.

These are three essential characteristics of Pugwash which we must build on: scientific eminence, independence and a spirit of friendship and trust. If we can do this, I do believe we have a future, and we can achieve our objectives.

Robert Reford:

It seems to me that there are basically two types of non-governmental organizations, one which tries to work inside, and one which tries to work outside. The one which tries to work inside, works to influence governments directly by getting in touch with the appropriate officials and political leaders. Those that operate outside try to influence governments indirectly by generating public pressures, mass movements, and public support. These two types of organization can, and indeed should, complement each other, but it may well be a mistake for any one organization to try to do both things, because being structured to be effective in one area does not necessarily qualify an organization to be effective in the other.

Now, if we consider what kind of an organization Pugwash is, I would start by noting some of the points which Joe Rotblat made. Pugwash is in a sense a "coalition of individuals." We come here as individuals most of whom are associated with some other kind of organization, but we don't come here to represent that organization. Coming to Pugwash as individuals, we learn what we can from our colleagues and exchange ideas, and then go back to our own particular groups, whether they be academic groups or protest groups, to spread the Pugwash message within those groups. That, it seems to me, is how Pugwash has operated, and is probably the way that Pugwash should continue to operate. Now of course organizations can change, and there may be those who think we should change, but, if so, I think that should be discussed at some future meeting, as for example in Warsaw.

But for now, I think that Pugwash has been an inside organization, and perhaps at the moment we would be better off to continue to try to be an effective inside organization.

Should Pugwash Extend its Role and Activities?

Paul Cappon:

What I have to say comes from the background I have in medical science, social science, and also from being involved very much in the popular disarmament movement. From that perspective I would like to talk about the relationship between disarmament and Pugwash and other non-governmental organizations. I have great sympathy for what Prof. Rotblat had to say, but I also think that what all non-governmental organizations have to offer is a great deal of courage as well as a means of influencing governments.

There has been some surprise as well as satisfaction, expressed here about the scope and extent of the popular disarmanent movement. The fact that there have been so many mass demonstrations has perhaps been surprising to some scientists because they have lived so long with technological evolution, which, even now that its pace is accelerated, is steady. The pattern of sudden visibility of the popular disarmament movement shows a very different trend, whose pattern is not surprising in terms of sociological analysis.

There have also been calls here to build on the mobilization of public opinion which has taken place. I feel very strongly that this mobilization has now reached a peak, and that it requires some concrete results in order to be sustained. There is a risk that the current US-USSR negotiations will become the great tranquilizer and that public disillusion and apathy may set in. My interest in this discussion is to discover what a distinguished body may do to lead and to keep the hope for disarmament alive. I feel that without this support, a partial collapse of the disarmament movement and the related processes would be quite likely.

When Mr. MacGuigan came here yesterday, he gave a speech which may indicate that if the popular movement has not had much effect on governmental policy it is not likely that scientific groups will either. However, I feel that there is one way a scientific group might have an impact on disarmament decision making.

What we can do is to provide a focus and leadership for the mass movement, without actually becoming its leaders. I think we can and should provide the detailed scientific analysis which the mass movement needs. In that context, my last point is that I don't see why, while supporting the freeze proposal, we cannot also set up a committee to prepare a detailed scientific document in support of the freeze proposal to show its merits or demerits.

William Epstein:

It was very illuminating to hear Joe Rotblat talk about the origins and history of Pugwash. However he made one statement which I did not understand. He said at the beginning of his talk that somebody had suggested that we become a mass movement or public forum. I was Chairman all day yesterday and I don't recall any person making that sort of proposal. I would have opposed that had I heard it. I wasn't in the room all day today, so I may have missed something.

I've always believed, and I still believe that all our discussions ought to be held in private, but that once we have reached a conclusion we need to communicate our views, not just to governments and to God, but to the public. They need our views. I recall in the 1950s that some scientists, some working for the government, and some not, came out with a report that the radiation from nuclear tests in the atmosphere was no more dangerous than the luminous dial of a wristwatch. Some other scientists, however, did some work showing that the milk teeth of children had a lot more radioactivity than had been believed. That helped galvanize the mothers of America. It was the mothers of America and of other countries and not the scientists who forced the governments to stop testing in the atmosphere. But they needed the information and expertise provided by the scientists.

I mentioned earlier the petition by thousands of scientists initiated by Linus Pauling calling for an end to nuclear testing. Dag Hammarskjold regarded that petition and its impact on the public and on governments as a big breakthrough.

In other words, it is the scientists working with the public that can achieve something. We do not have to nor should we become a mass movement, or even lead it, but we can provide it with guidance and, in that sense, leadership. But scientists talking to other scientists are not really doing the job they should do unless they also reach out to the public and to governments. A number of speakers before me have urged that Pugwash should make its scientific expertise available to the public and thus provide leadership.

I was rather disappointed after the Banff Conference, which clearly called for a nuclear freeze, that its message was not even sent to many governments. I called a number of officials in the United States—in the Arms Control and Disarmament Agency, and the State Department, and also several Senators, and I found that not one of them had been sent a copy of the Council Statement issued after the Banff Conference. So I asked Senator Charles Percy, who was one of the invited guests at the public forum held in Calgary as part of the Banff conference, if he would consider inserting the Banff Pugwash Statement in the Congressional Record. I am happy to say that he did. I also arranged for the printing of 20,000 copies of the Banff Statement which we arranged to go to every member of the United Nations and was also sent far and wide throughout the land with the help of a number of organizations. My point is that, once we do arrive at a public statement, it is very important that we should spread the message. Unfortunately, that isn't always done by Pugwash. A number of members of the Canadian Group don't even get the Newsletter which is supposed to go to all Pugwashites.

As regards the three points mentioned by Rotblat, I fully agree that Pugwash must have eminent scientists, and independence, and that trust and friendship among us, is important. I would like to add a fourth point which I think is essential. It is that Pugwash has a duty to help inform and educate the governments and peoples of the world and not merely other scientists.

I certainly agree that Pugwash is and must be a channel between East and West. And Pugwash scientists should go to the Pugwash Conference in Warsaw next month because one of our jobs is to communicate between East and West. Even when things are difficult we should communicate.

So to sum up, I agree with everything that has been said about the role of Pugwash as an independent channel for eminent scientists who must meet and work in a spirit of trust. I would only add that, once Pugwash has agreed on a position, it is our duty to reach out and communicate our ideas to the governments and peoples of the world. In fact we agreed to that yesterday when we all approved the 25th Anniversary Declaration by the Canadian Pugwash Group.

Rod Byers:

I do agree with Bill Epstein's fourth point, and I also agree with the three points which were made by Joe Rotblat. However, I would just add that, when one educates and informs the governments and the public, I would hope it will continue to be in the tradition of Pugwash, and that is that it will be based on sound research. Our statements should be an attempt to be at the leading edge of the debate. We should extend the debate a step further. I would say that the Chemical Workshop efforts by Pugwash very much fit into that category, as is the case with a lot of other things that Pugwash does. We have to continue to maintain that tradition, which is why I think we should have an Ad Hoc Working Group on the Freeze at Warsaw so there can be a more detailed statement on the implications of the freeze.

Bernard Feld:

I agree with almost everything that has been said. I certainly would not propose that Pugwash hide its light under a barrel. Our objective is to spread light as far as possible. Nevertheless, every group has a natural constituency. I think we must remember that the natural constituency of Pugwash is the world scientific community. Thus this is the group to which we speak in the first instance, and this is the group to involve in our work in the first instance. Anything beyond that is fine, it's great. But we have to remember who our primary constituency is and really focus on the most effective way of building this constituency in directions which we think are important.

John Polanyi:

I wish to underline one point that was just made, and also address the question raised earlier by Frank Sommers as to whether our intellectual work was mainly based on rationalization. I would say such work is really useful. There is a huge debate that goes on regarding the technology of weapons systems, which has a great deal to do with the continuation of the arms race. The people who are involved in that debate are entitled to be informed in the terms in which they ask their questions. I mean if they are to be told that the arms race is all nonsense, they must be told in ways they can understand. That means that we must come to grips with the technicalities which are brandished by those supporting the arms race. This has traditionally been one of the roles of Pugwash. The idea of Pugwash from the beginning was to have a constituency of people who were not directly involved in military matters, but who could understand our arguments. In fact when the US Arms Control and Disarmament Agency was created, there was a question raised in Pugwash as to whether Pugwash had become superfluous. Of course one has only to look at the Arms Control and Disarmament Agency today to realize that this is not the case. There is still a need for that constituency to be nourished, and Pugwash is in a good position to do it.

K. Subrahmanyan:

I think a review of the history of Pugwash, will reveal that it was established at a time when there was very deep anxiety about weapons of mass destruction. From about the late 1960s until about two or three years ago there was a period of detente and there were a certain number of arms control agreements. I have a feeling that that was also reflected in Pugwash in that the sense of urgency tended to decline with direct US-Soviet negotiations, with growing detente and with the number of arms control agreements achieved. So I think that the idea of the public being tranquilized is at least partially correct.

There is no difficulty in accepting Joe Rotblat's three points, and also Bill Epstein's fourth point, but there is a connection between the two. When we are talking about informing and educating, it is important to remember that ultimately Pugwash is its members. For example, if Dr. Linus Pauling makes a statement, that makes news. In contrast, a statement from Pugwash, in spite of its prestige, will attract somewhat less attention. It is the individual outstanding members of Pugwash that are able to have greater impact on the media than does Pugwash as a group itself. Consequently the point about increasing participation in Pugwash by eminent and prestigious scientists is a necessary prerequisite of the work to inform and educate. Thus we have the frequent heartbreaking experience of the media not taking notice of Pugwash statements. But the same thing, if said by one of our leading members, such as a Nobel Laureate, would attract attention.

Therefore the question of informing and educating should be linked up now with a drive to bring leading members of the scientific community into Pugwash.

I think that today we are in a period of crisis which is similar to the second half of the 50s. In those days it was fear of surprise attack; now there is a widespread fear of a nuclear war. Consequently, I am quite sure that even those eminent scientists who might not have bothered to join Pugwash 2 or 3 years ago, may do so now because of the present climate.

There are several other categories of people we should approach, including former commanders of nuclear forces who have come out against nuclear weapons and former policy makers who have now turned against nuclear weapons. It is important that we contact these people as well as physicists, chemists and biochemists.

On the question of our relationship to mass movements, as has been said, it is for the individuals to go and take part in the mass movements, to energize them and to bring Pugwash ideas and expertise to these movements. And of course, as we all agree, Pugwash itself cannot be converted into a mass organization. I think everyone who has spoken thinks that it is important to preserve our identity as an independent body that works in private but whose ideas should be public and publicized.

Lastly, I would also say that it will take more than a few years and we should recognize that a broadly based struggle will be necessary to delegitimize nuclear war. This will only happen when the streets are full of people. If you look at two or three major precedents where established ideas have been delegitimized, such as colonialism, color prejudice, segregation, or apartheid, it has taken decades to change people's views, and in the case of slavery it took centuries. Now to delegitimize nuclear weapons is going to take quite some time. And ultimately the struggle is not going to be in Pugwash. The struggle is going to be in the streets, but we can be among the energizers and provide the leadership of ideas. That is all that we can do.

Derek Paul:

As regards the question of what Pugwash should be doing to help mobilize pulic opinion, I think that one of the reasons Pugwash has not done all of the things we say are needed is quite clearly because it is too small. Two thousand scientists in 75 countries cannot possible do the tasks that have been suggested today without an enormous army of helpers. There was a clear idea along these lines in Canada when Science for Peace was formed. It was felt that the Pugwash Movement is too small and that Science for Peace could make good that defect by building a much larger organization, which tries to do these other tasks which are beyond the power of the tiny handful of Pugwash scientists in any given country.

I want to add something to the point made by Bernard Feld to the effect that our constituency is the scientists. I do think that this an area in which Pugwash has not been succeeding as well we should.

There is an enormous difference between the Pugwash groups in different countries. In England, the group known as Friends of Pugwash plays a very useful role in communicating with the public and with scientists. In Canada, about a year ago, we started an organization called "Science for Peace" which was set up deliberately to cooperate with Pugwash. This group, is better able to communicate with other scientists than the Canadian Pugwash Group because it is larger. I am not aware of any such group in the United States. In the German federal Republic they have the Vereinigung Deutscher Wissenschafter which plays that role.

Thus an auxilary organization or non-profit corporation could be a valuable asset for our work to supplement Pugwash itself which is and should remain small.

Sergei Kapitza:

I would like to support what Joe Rotblat has said. To implement his objective of attracting increasingly eminent scientists, it would seem important to choose our priorities in a more deliberate way. It is my feeling that we often try to solve too many problems and thus dissipate our potential and our efforts. I think it is important to concentrate on the right questions if we are to reach our full potential constituency.

I think another problem in reaching the world scientific community is due to the apathy that people feel toward work that manifests itself just in words. People who are used to action cannot understand how one can argue about minutiae when everything is going wrong. It is like arguing about what color flag to put up when the ship is sinking. In the European Physical Society I have noted some of the same problems.

We need to consider how we can support these words by deeds, and also examine how words can change the behavior and attitudes of people. I have not been able to get a coherent explanation of the recent mass demonstrations. It is a subject that deserves study, maybe after some time we will gain an understanding of what happened and what were the decisive factors. To what extent it is a cumulative build up, and what was the contribution of different politicians to this phenomenon, are examples of the questions to ask.

Our efforts in educating and in disseminating our message must be connected to the way it really does have maximum effect. This is a question which it would be worth discussing in a workshop on the mass media. These are points which could be discussed in Warsaw.

Sir Mark Oliphant:

I want to draw people's attention to something that was done by Benjamin Franklin. He founded a group in Philadelphia to discuss the problems of his time, and he imposed on the members an oath which can be expressed in these words:

> We swear diligently to seek the truth, and having found it, to impart it to others.

Now I think that second part is all important. Pugwash should follow it.

Lucy Webster:

I wish to reinforce the comments that have been made to the effect that Pugwash should assume a leadership role, not only for scientists, but also for a broader public. This can be done both by individual Pugwash scientists and by group statements and publications. Leadership is needed to guide and give confidence to the mass movements not only to encourage work for disarmament but to help to de-legitimize war, and especially nuclear war.

Finally, I hope Pugwash will continue working to create the sort of cohesive and cogent information base that will help to guide public debate and action. We need a document setting out the technical and other military-political considerations, we need a more comprehensive study of each of the main issues such as the nuclear freeze and no-first-use. This could help to provide leadership for the whole mass movement. And I hope that Pugwash will continue to contribute to that leadership task.

19. THE DECLARATION

AND THE LINUS PAULING STATEMENT

Chairman:

We have heard several times that what we need are scientists of outstanding stature. Well I feel we have succeeded in getting them here to this meeting of the Canadian Pugwash Group.

We shall send both the Declaration that we adopted here and the Statement initiated by Linus Pauling to the Warsaw Pugwash Conference for consideration there.

I want to thank all of you for having come and for making this meeting the success it has been. We hope that it will help promote the work and aims of Pugwash on *both* the Canadian and the international scene.

This meeting is in the tradition of the Canadian Pugwash Movement. We in Canada have tried to inform the people and the Government. We think we have helped influence the Canadian Government to become more active in the field of disarmament. We intend to continue to reach out to members of Parliament, and to other scientists and also to NGOs and the public. That, we think, is the right role for Pugwash.

DECLARATION

BY THE CANADIAN PUGWASH GROUP

on the 25th Anniversary of the holding of
the First Pugwash Conference at Pugwash, Canada,
in July 1957

A quarter of a century ago a small group of 22 distinguished scientists from 10 East-West countries assembled in Pugwash, Nova Scotia, on the invitation of Mr. Cyrus Eaton, to seek ways of ending the Cold War, preventing a hot war and avoiding a nuclear holocaust. They were inspired by the Russell-Einstein Manifesto pointing to the dangers of a nuclear war that could put an end to the human race.

That meeting gave its name to the Pugwash Movement which has spread around the world and now encompasses some 2000 scientists from 75 countries.

Today, on the invitation of Canadian Pugwash, another small group of scientists, including signers of the Russell-Einstein Manifesto and participants in the first Pugwash Conference, have gathered in Pugwash to commemorate the 25th Anniversary of that first meeting. There follows the statement adopted by the Canadian Pugwash Group.

The nuclear peril facing the nations and the peoples of the world is now much greater than it was 25 years ago. Nine multilateral treaties and thirteen bilateral American-Soviet treaties and agreements on arms limitation have failed to halt the arms race which continues to escalate. The arms race, and in particular the nuclear arms race, is proceeding in a more dangerous way than ever before. The threat it poses to human survival knows no parallel in all history.

Increasing numbers of scientists and the public realize that peace and security cannot be found in the vast and

- 157 -

continuing accumulation of weapons of destruction or in the current concepts of deterrence. Unfortunately, however, others, including some in positions of authority, speak of fighting, surviving and even winning a limited nuclear war, a protracted nuclear war or an all-out nuclear war. We believe that these illusions verge on insanity and can only lead to a mad race to oblivion.

We agree with and fully support the declaration of 1978 of the United Nations General Assembly's First Special Session on Disarmament:

> Removing the threat of world war—a nuclear war—is the most acute and urgent task of the present day. Mankind is confronted with a choice: we must halt the arms race and proceed to disarmament or face annihilation.

There now exist some 50,000 nuclear weapons whose destructive power is more than one million times greater than the bomb that destroyed Hiroshima. Not only is the number of weapons increasing but, what is worse, the nuclear arms race is now mainly a qualitative race rather than a quantitative one. The rapid pace of technological innovation and the development of new, more accurate and more devastating weapon systems so far exceeds the slow pace of arms control and disarmament negotiations as to make a mockery of the efforts to halt and reverse the arms race. The threat of nuclear annihilation, either by design or as a result of accident, desperation, miscalculation, or panic, grows greater year by year.

In these circumstances, the only sure way of halting the nuclear arms race is by freezing the testing, production and deployment of all nuclear weaons and their delivery vehicles by the two superpowers. Such a freeze is a necessary first step to major reductions in the stock piles of these weapons and toward the goal of their eventual elimination. Indeed, a reduction in the number of nuclear weapons and their delivery systems, without a freeze, could be meaningless. The modernization of older weapon systems and the development of even more horrible and threatening new ones could completely negate the effect of any reduction in numbers. A technological freeze is as necessary as numerical reductions, and even more urgent. Moreover, if small nuclear delivery vehicles, such as cruise missiles, are produced and deployed in large numbers, it will be extremely difficult, if not impossible, to verify their limitation and reduction. Thus, time is indeed running out on efforts to halt and reverse the nuclear arms race.

Recently there have been several hopeful developments as people all over the world have become alerted to the dangers of the nuclear arms race. Millions have rallied to demand a stop to the arms race, and a great human cry for a nuclear freeze is surging around the world.

Another hopeful development is the growing demand that additional Governments pledge not to be the first to use nuclear weapons.* Declarations of no-first-use by all the nuclear weapon powers would be tantamount to declarations never to use these weapons. We believe that any imbalance in conventional forces is not of such dimensions as to prevent the making of no-first-use pledges; the making of such pledges, however, could be more readily agreed to if there were agreement on mutual balanced conventional forces in Europe.

It is also encouraging that several scientific inventors of some of the most sophisticated nuclear weapons systems ever conceived by the mind of man now oppose their use and urge their abolition.

In the light of these developments, we believe that the scientists of the world—and particularly those who are members of the Pugwash Movement—have a duty to help inform and educate the governments and peoples of the world about the dangers of the nuclear arms race and to explore ways of improving international security in order to avoid a nuclear war.

The members of the Canadian Pugwash Movement and the distinguished guests invited to join them at this 25th Anniversary Commemorative Meeting at Pugwash, Canada,

---

*Such pledges were made by China in 1964 and by the USSR during the Second UN Special Session on Disarmament in 1982.

call on the Pugwash Movement and the scientists of the world to intensify their efforts and to rededicate their energies and activities to the abolition of the threat of nuclear war and to the establishment of a just and secure world order.

STATEMENT

initiated by Dr. Linus Pauling

at Pugwash, N.S.

The danger of world destruction in a nuclear war is now greater than ever before because of the escalating arms race between the United States and the Soviet Union. To halt this race, we urge that the USSR and the USA undertake through either simultaneous national declarations or a joint declaration to freeze the testing, production, and deployment of all nuclear weaons and their delivery vehicles, with the freeze to be followed by major reductions.

APPENDIX 1

The Russell-Einstein Manifesto

issued in London, July 9th 1955

In the tragic situation which confronts humanity, we feel that scientists should assemble in conference to appraise the perils that have arisen as a result of the development of weapons of mass destruction, and to discuss a resolution in the spirit of the appended draft.

We are speaking on this occasion, not as members of this or that nation, continent, or creed, but as human beings, members of the species Man, whose continued existence is in doubt. The world is full of conflicts; and, overshadowing all minor conflicts, the titanic struggle between Communism and anti-Communism.

Almost everybody who is politically conscious has strong feelings about one or more of these issues; but we want you, if you can, to set aside such feelings and consider yourselves only as members of a biological species which has had a remarkable history, and whose disappearance none of us can desire.

We shall try to say no single word which should appeal to one group rather than to another. All, equally, are in peril, and, if the peril is understood, there is hope that they may collectively avert it.

We have to learn to think in a new way. We have to learn to ask ourselves, not what steps can be taken to give military victory to whatever group we prefer, for there no longer are such steps; the question we have to ask ourselves is: what steps can be taken to prevent a military contest of which the issue must be disastrous to all parties?

The general public, and even many men in positions of authority, have not realized what would be involved in a war with nuclear bombs. The general public still thinks in terms of the obliteration of cities. It is understood that the new bombs are more powerful than the old, and that, while one A-bomb could obliterate Hiroshima, one H-bomb could obliterate the largest cities, such as London, New York, and Moscow.

No doubt in an H-bomb war great cities would be obliterated. But this is one of the minor disasters that would have to be faced. If everybody in London, New York and Moscow were exterminated, the world might, in the course of a few centuries, recover from the blow. But we now know, especially since the Bikini test, that nuclear bombs can gradually spread destruction over a very much wider area than had been supposed.

It is stated on very good authority that a bomb can now be manufactured which will be 2,500 times as powerful as that which destroyed Hiroshima. Such a bomb, if exploded near the ground or under water, sends radio-active particles into the upper air. They sink gradually and reach the surface of the earth in the form of a deadly dust or rain. It was this dust which infected the Japanese fishermen and their catch of fish.

No one knows how widely such lethal radio-active particles might be diffused, but the best authorities are unanimous in saying that a war with H-bombs might possibly put an end to the human race. It is feared that if many H-bombs are used there will be universal death— sudden only for a minority, but for the majority a slow torture of disease and disintegration.

Many warnings have been uttered by eminent men of science and by authorities in military strategy. None of them will say that the worst results are certain. What they do say is that these results are possible, and no one can be sure that they will not be realized. We have not yet found that the views of experts on this question depend in any degree upon their politics or prejudices. They depend only, so far as our researches have revealed, upon the extent of the particular expert's knowledge. We have found that the men who know most are the most gloomy.

Here, then, is the problem which we present to you, stark and dreadful and inescapable: Shall we put an end to the human race; or shall mankind renounce war? People will not face this alternative because it is so difficult to abolish war.

The abolition of war will demand distasteful limitations of national sovereignty. But what perhaps impedes understanding of the situation more than anything else is that the term "mankind" feels vague and abstract. People scarcely realize in imagination that the danger is to themselves and their children and their grandchildren, and not only to a dimly apprehended humanity. They can scarcely bring themselves to grasp that they, individually, and those whom they love are in imminent danger of perishing agonizingly. And so they hope that perhaps war may be allowed to continue provided modern weapons are prohibited.

This hope is illusory. Whatever agreements not to use H-bombs had been reached in time of peace, they would no longer be considered binding in time of war, and both sides would set to work to manufacture H-bombs as soon as war broke out, for, if one side manufactured the bombs and the other did not, the side that manufactured them would inevitably be victorious.

Although an agreement to renounce nuclear weapons as part of a general reduction of armaments would not afford an ultimate solution, it would serve certain important purposes. First: any agreement between East and West is to the good in so far as it tends to diminish tension. Second: the abolition of thermo-nuclear weapons, if each side believed that the other had carried it out sincerely, would lessen the fear of a sudden attack in the style of Pearl Harbour, which at present keeps both sides in a state of nervous apprehension. We should, therefore, welcome such an agreement, though only as a first step.

Most of us are not neutral in feeling, but, as human beings, we have to remember that, if the issues between East and West are to be decided in any manner that can give any possible satisfaction to anybody, whether Communist or anti-Communist, whether Asian or European or American, whether White or Black, then these issues must

- 165 -

not be decided by war. We should wish this to be understood, both in the East and in the West.

There lies before us, if we choose, continual progress in happiness, knowledge, and wisdom. Shall we, instead, choose death, because we cannot forget our quarrels? We appeal, as human beings, to human beings: Remember your humanity, and forget the rest. If you can do so, the way lies open to a new Paradise; if you cannot, there lies before you the risk of universal death.

Resolution

We invite this Congress, and through it the scientists of the world and the general public, to subscribe to the following resolution:

In view of the fact that in any future world war nuclear weapons will certainly be employed, and that such weapons threaten the continued existence of mankind, we urge the Governments of the world to realize, and to acknowledge publicly, that their purpose cannot be furthered by a world war, and we urge them, consequently, to find peaceful means for the settlement of all matters of dispute between them.

Max Born	Linus Pauling
Percy W. Bridgman	Cecil F. Powell
Albert Einstein	Joseph Rotblat
Leopold Infeld	Bertrand Russell
Frederic Joliot-Curie	Hideki Yukawa
Herman J. Muller	

APPENDIX 2

MEMO TO: W. Epstein
FROM: K. Tsipis
RE: Weaponization of outer space
DATE: July 8, 1982

Here are some points that may prove useful during your discussions at Pugwash:

1.   Outer space has already been militarized in the sense that it is used for a multiplicity of military applications and functions. All these, however, are "force multiplier" uses in the sense that they support and improve the performance of Earth-based systems.

2.   There are three types of satellites, two types of potential antisatellite systems, and two ways to exclude antisatellite activities in space.

The three types of satellites are:
   i.   Near Earth orbit (200-1000 km)
  ii.   Intermediate orbit (20,000 km)
 iii.   Geosynchronous orbit (40,000 km).

Monitoring and other satellites used to oversee military activities or preparations on land are in near-Earth orbits.

Communications, weather and navigations satellites are in intermediate orbits.

Additional—important—communications and early warning satellites are in geosynchronous orbits.

The two types of potential antisatellite systems are:
   i.   Dedicated systems, developed and deployed to perform antisatellite missions.
  ii.   Non-dedicated satellites or vehicles with marginal or ancillary antisatellite capabilities.

The Soviet co-orbiting ASAT system and the US direct ascent ASAT system now under development (first test in October 1982) fall in the first category.

The US space shuttle and probably other satellites fall in the second category.

The two possible approaches towards banning ASAT activities in space are:

i. Sign a formal treaty banning the testing, deployment and use of dedicated ASAT systems.

ii. Devise "rules of the road" that will insure that non-dedicated systems will not be used to interfere with the function of satellites.

3. Current situation.

The Soviet Union has been testing a co-orbiting system capable of attacking low-orbit US satellites as well as the Space Shuttle. The system is expensive and awkward and less than 50% of its tests were considered "successful." The system can be improved to reach higher orbits, including geosynchronous, but it would be extremely laborious, time-consuming and probably ineffective against intermediate- and geosynchronous-orbit satellites.

The US system consists of a 15-pound can filled with metallic shrapnel and equipped with an infrared homing device. It is mounted on a SHRAM missile which is mounted on a small sounding-rocket. The whole contraption is launched from an F-15 plane at high altitude. This system (miniature homing vehicle MHV) is much more cost-effective and easier to use than the Soviet system *if* it works as designed. It is much cheaper and much more technically sensible than the Soviet system. It can also only reach low-orbit satellites.

4. Exotic ASAT weapons.

A neutral particle beam or a laser weapon orbiting above the Earth could in principle attack and destroy satellites in proximate orbits. Neither of the two technologies are mature and neither lend themselves to anti-satellite applications, readily or with low technical risk.

Land-based lasers deployed on mountain tops could in principle damage satellites passing overhead. But they are operationally unpromising and awkward (you have to wait until the target passes overhead and then you don't have a chance to shoot at it, or another one, for quite a while) and they are weather-dependent. Deployment of such a system will have propaganda rather than operational military value. It will also be profoundly undesirable since it will most assuredly initiate fierce competition in anti-satellite systems.

Index

173

174

Laser weapons, 122
Leonard, James, xvii, 67, 70
Lewis, Flora, xvii, 128
Limited nuclear war
    1950s view of, 68
    and nuclear morality, 28

MacGuigan, Mark, xvii, 3, 7,
    145
Markov, M. A., 57, 61
Mass movements. See also Anti-
    nuclear movement; Public
    opinion
    need to explain, 153
    and Pugwash role, 151, 154
Media, use of, 87
Mexico
    Canadian agreement with, 15
    freeze resolution by, 110,
    127, 133
    leadership from, 81-82
Millionshchikov, M. P., 57
Moore-Ede, Martin, 38
Moratorium, unilateral, 38-40.
    See also Freeze on nuclear
    weapons
Morrison, Philip, 38
Morrison, Phylis, 38
Mühlhausen Pugwash Conference,
    55-56
Muller, Herman J., 49, 166
Muller, James, 46
Mutual assured destruction
    (MAD). See also Deterrence
    and morality, 28
    vs. NUTS, 51
Mutual balanced force reduction
    (MBFR), 12
Mutual national actions, for
    freeze, 107-108. See also
    Simultaneous approach, to
    freeze
Myrdal, Alva, vii

NATO, as freeze opponent, 93-94,
    95
Negotiations, disarmament
    blocking of, 133
    and freeze, 99, 131, 132,
    133
    frustration with, 139
    secrecy of, 98-90
"New Directions in Disarmament,"

Pugwash symposium on, 66
New Directions in Disaramament
    (Epstein and Feld), 66
New York Times, poll by, 119
NGOs (non-governmental
    organizations)
    inside vs. outside, 144
    and public opinion, 82,
    83-84
    and Pugwash Movement, 83
    and UN Secretariat, 75-76
    at UN Special Sessions, 76
    and World Disarmament
    Campaign, 78, 79
Noel-Baker, Philip, 33
No-first-use pledge
    effects of, xiii
    and freeze, 98, 104-105,
    109
    need for, 159
    Soviet, 20, 40, 63, 73, 101
    and UN session, xi
No More War (Pauling), 36-37
Non-nuclear weapons systems
    concern with, 13
    and nuclear freeze, 92
Non-Proliferation Treaty (NPT)
    (1968), xii, 15-16
    Canadian support of, 14
    and CTBT, 25
    and nuclear disarmament, 25,
    26
Nova Scotia Coalition Against
    Nuclear War, 85
NPT Review Conference, 25
Nuclear arms control. See
    Arms control
Nuclear arms race
    absurdity of, 29
    qualitative development of,
    96, 97, 158
Nuclear cooperation agreements,
    by Canada, 15
Nuclear disarmament. See
    Disarmament, nuclear
Nuclear freeze. See Freeze on
    nuclear weapons
Nuclear Illusion and Reality
    (Zuckerman), 24
Nuclear proliferation. See Non-
    Proliferation Treaty
Nuclear reduction
    and deterrence, 63
    as freeze sequel, 91, 93,
    98, 109

175

sabotage of, 89
and verification, 112
Satellites, types of, 167. See
also Anti-satellite weapons
Science
cooperative use of, 65-66
distrust of, 60
harmful use of, 138
spirit of, 36
Science for Peace, 151, 152
Scientists
in alliance with religious
leaders, 45-48
and first strike, 100
and freeze, 97-98
and politicians, 57-58
and public opinion, 146-147
Pugwash as movement of,
141-142, 147-148, 149, 150,
151-152
responsibility of, 43, 50,
118, 119
Scientists on the Arms Race
and Disarmament, 142
Scoville, Herbert Jr., xviii,
89, 90, 96, 111, 113, 129
Second Special Session on
Disarmament, UN, x-xi, 7,
8-9
Canadian efforts on, 84
differeing opinions on, 73
disappointment over, 84
and disarmament/development
report, 30
freeze resolution introduced
at, xi, 26, 110
Gromyko's remarks at, 13
NGOs at, 76
and peace movements, 31
and proliferation, 14
results of, 23, 24, 26
Soviet no-first-use
declaration at, 20, 73
Subramanyam comments on,
82-83
World Disarmament Campaign
from, 34, 73-74, 75-77
(see also World Disarmament
Campaign)
Secrecy
government misuse of, 89-90
and war feasibility, 54
Seismic data, for verification,
14, 44

Selove, Walter, 49
Simultaneous approach, to
freeze, 112, 114, 127
Stockholm International Peace
Research Institute (SIPRI),
83
Smaller countries
critical role of, 68
technology-paying proposal
for, 54-55
"Small" nuclear weapons,
European deployment of,
67-68
Social responsibility, of
scientists, 43, 50, 118,
119
Sommaripa, George, 38
Sommers, Frank, xix, 84, 117,
138, 149
Soviet Military Power (U.S.
government), 94-95
Soviet Pugwash Group, 62
Soviet Union. See also United
States-Soviet Union
relationship
Council on problems of peace
and disarmament of, 61-62
and first strike, 100
on fissionable-material
production ban, 128
and freeze, 20, 92-93,
105-106
no-first-use declaration by,
20, 40, 63, 73, 101
and outer space ban, 123
TV nuclear discussion in, 60
at UNSSOD II, 20, 73
Space exploration, cooperative
pursuit of, 65
START Talks, xii, 69
and freeze, xiii, 101-102
secrecy of, 89, 90
U.S. position in, 10-11
Statement of Linus Pauling,
114-115, 115-116, 126, 127,
134, 135, 137, 155, 161
Subrahmanyan, K., xix, 82, 86,
100, 150
Suffocation strategy
and innovation, 132
Trudeau calls for, 8-9
Superiority, nuclear
absurdity of, x, 98
need to address, 100

About the Editors

WILLIAM EPSTEIN is a Special Fellow of UNITAR and a consultant on Disarmament to the U.N. Secretary-General and the Canadian Government. He was Director of the Disarmament Division of the U.N. for a number of years. He is a Senior Research Associate at Carleton Univeristy, Ottawa, and has been a Visiting Professor at several Canadian and American Universities. He was a member of the Canadian Delegation to six sessions of the U.S. General Assembly. He was Chairman of the International Group of Experts which prepared the report on Chemical and Biological Weapons (1969), and a member of the Group which prepared the Report on a Comprehensive Test Ban (1980) for the United Nations. He was Technical Consultant to the Commission which prepared the Treaty of Tlatelolco, which created a Nuclear Free Zone in Latin America. He has represented the U.N. Secretary-General at a number of disarmament conferences. He is the Chairman of the Canadian Pugwash Group. He is the author of The Last Chance: Nuclear Proliferation and Arms Control, and has published extensively in the field of disarmament and international security.

LUCY WEBSTER is a Director of the Institute for Global Policy Studies which has its headquarters in Amsterdam; it undertakes research on the development of the world political system especially as this relates to the United Nations. She has worked as a political and economic research analyst in London, Amsterdam, Geneva and New York, where she has also been a consultant at the United Nations. She is Executive Chairman of the World Association of World Federalists.